German Shepherd Dogs

SUSAN M. EWING

German Shepherd Dogs
In Interpet Book

Project Team
Editor: Heather Russell-Revesz
Copy Editor: Ellen Fusz
Design: Stephanie Krautheim
Design Layout: Angela Stanford

First published in UK in 2007 by
Interpet Publishing
Vincent Lane
Dorking
Surrey
RH4 3YX

ISBN: 978 1 84286 159 2

Printed and bound in China

This book has been published with the intent to provide accurate and authoritative information in regard to the subject matter within. While every precaution has been taken in preparation of this book, the author and publisher expressly disclaim responsibility for any errors, omissions, or adverse effects arising from the use or application of the information contained herein. The techniques and suggestions are used at the reader's discretion and are not to be considered a substitute for veterinary care. If you suspect a medical problem consult your vet.

www.interpet.co.uk

Table of Contents

Chapter 1

Why I Adore My German Shepherd Dog.....................5
History • Today's GSD • The Look of the GSD • Living With a GSD

Chapter 2

The Stuff of Everyday Life............................15
Crate • Dog Bed • Ex-pen • Food and Water Bowls • Gate •
Grooming Tools • Identification • Collar and Lead • Toys

Chapter 3

Good Eating..25
Commercial Diets • Non-commercial Options • Variety Is the Spice of
Life • Free Feeding or Scheduled Feeding? • Obesity

Chapter 4

Looking Good......................................39
Brushing • Bathing • Ear Care • Eye Care • Nail Care • Dental Care •
Groomers • Accessories

Chapter 5

Feeling Good......................................51
Finding a Vet • Puppy's First Visit • Yearly Check-ups • Vaccinations •
Potential Health Issues for the GSD • Other Common Issues • First Aid •
Holistic Therapies

Chapter 6

Being Good..69
Socialisation • Housetraining • Basic Commands • Tricks

Chapter 7

In the Doghouse...................................83
Barking (Excessive) • Chewing • Digging • Housetraining accidents •
Jumping Up • Nipping • Finding a Behaviourist

Chapter 8

Stepping Out......................................93
Travelling With Your GSD • Sports and Other Activities

Resources..104
Index...109

Chapter 1

Why I Adore My

German Shepherd Dog

German Shepherd Dogs are one of the most versatile breeds in existence. The German Shepherd is willing and able to "do it all," whether herding a flock of sheep, guarding a home or business, using that sensitive nose to sniff out drugs or bombs, leading the blind, assisting the disabled, earning titles in the show ring, or just being a family companion. Ask the German Shepherd Dog to do something, and he's up to the challenge.

History

The German Shepherd Dog (GSD to his friends) was originally a farm dog, guarding the flocks and herds of the family. Unlike some herding breeds, which were bred to move animals from one area to another, the GSD was bred to patrol a boundary—keeping the flock inside and all intruders outside of a given area.

In the late 1800s Captain Max von Stephanitz of Germany developed the modern-day German Shepherd Dog. He admired the all-purpose working dog but was afraid that, as flocks and farms diminished, the breed would eventually disappear. He created an official governing body for the breed, and then developed the *schutzhund trial* as a way of determining a dog's ability to work. If a dog failed to pass a schutzhund test, he could not be bred. A schutzhund test comprises many of the elements of today's working trials, with the dog obeying commands to sit, stand, and stay, as well as retrieve, jump, and scale walls. A schutzhund trial also includes a section where a dog attacks on command. The result of von Stephanitz's strict requirements led to the intelligent, versatile German Shepherd Dog of today.

The herding and guarding instinct is still present in today's GSD, even though few of them are called upon to tend a flock. Instead, their family becomes their flock. A German Shepherd may nip at the heels of running children and may even take a hand gently in his mouth to lead a person in what he considers the correct direction.

Today's GSD

The German Shepherd Dog first came to the UK following World War I, and was registered by the Kennel Club in 1919. The American Kennel Club registered its first GSD in 1908. The German Shepherd Dog's popularity soared in the 1920s and 30s with Hollywood's help. Films starring German Shepherd Dogs showcased their intelligence and everyone, it seemed, wanted their own Rin Tin Tin.

The Look of the GSD

What should your wonderful German Shepherd Dog look like? Kennel clubs develop written breed standards that describe the "ideal" dog. According to the KC standard, a Shepherd should be an "alert, powerful, well-muscled animal. His

working ability should be immediately apparent. A GSD is slightly longer than tall, and the individual should give a clear impression of masculinity or femininity."

Size

The ideal size for females is 23 inches (58.5 cm) at the shoulders, and for males 25 inches (62.5 cm) tall.

Coat

GSDs have double coats to protect them from all weather. There's a soft, fluffy undercoat to keep the dog warm and a harsher, longer outer coat that sheds water, snow, and dirt. The coat is medium length with shorter hair on the head, legs,

The Expert Knows

The First Guide Dog

One of the first guide dogs in the US was a GSD. In 1927, Dorothy Harrison Eustis wrote an article on GSDs trained to lead the blind in Switzerland. A young blind man named Morris Frank, inspired by the article, went to Switzerland to train with Dorothy Eustis and a female German Shepherd Dog named Buddy. Together, Morris, Dorothy, and a few others, developed the first dog guide school in America, and their work was instrumental in founding the Guide Dogs for the Blind Association in the UK.

A Shepherd has a noble head and almond shaped dark eyes.

and paws, and slightly longer hair around the neck.

Colour

While it's true that "a good dog can't be a bad colour" most breed standards mention colour preferences. With the German Shepherd, strong, rich colours are preferred, and white is not recognised in the show ring.

Head

A Shepherd has a noble head and a keen, intelligent and composed expression, with almond shaped dark eyes. The ears are carried erect, and they open toward the front. As described in the KC standard, the forehead should have a slight curve, and should blend into a long, strong muzzle effortlessly.

Body

A Shepherd has a large chest that is carried well down between the legs. This allows ample room for the dog's lungs and heart. The ribs are "well-sprung and long," and allow the dogs front legs to move freely. "Well-sprung" ribs are the ideal between flat, or slab-sided, and round. If the ribs are too flat, there's not as much room for the lungs to fully expand. If the ribs are too round they interfere with the legs, throwing the elbows out and making the gait less efficient. That means the dog will tire more quickly and not be able to work as long.

Movement

Watch your dog as he plays in the garden. Watch him move when you call him. The chances are you'll see him trotting—that's what he's supposed to do. A German Shepherd Dog is a trotting dog, and his structure has been developed to meet the requirements of his work. The movement of the GSD is so important that the standard describes exactly how this athletic dog should move. In essence, his gait should be elastic, seemingly without effort, smooth and rhythmic, and covering the maximum amount of ground with the minimum number of steps. He should have the coordination and balance so that his gait appears to be the steady motion of a well-lubricated machine. The feet travel close to the ground on both forward reach and backward push. In order to achieve ideal movement of this kind, there must be good muscular development and ligamentation. The GSD's back must have great strength to pull off the typical smooth, flowing gait.

Temperament

The Kennel Club (KC) says this about the temperament of the German Shepherd Dog: "Steady of nature, loyal, self-assured, courageous and tractable. Never nervous, over-aggressive or shy. The German Shepherd has an impeccable temperament; it is a hallmark of the breed." A German Shepherd will accept family friends, but he is rarely effusive in his greetings. His loyalty and devotion is to his family, and all others come in a distant second.

SENIOR DOG TIP

Senior GSD

Somewhere between the ages of seven and ten, your German Shepherd Dog may start to slow down a bit. You may notice that your dog seems a bit stiff when he gets up after a nap. He may not want to play fetch for as long a time. Your dog's muzzle may start to turn grey. None of this means that you and your dog can't still enjoy lots of activities, but it does mean that you'll want to pay attention to when your dog is tired. Talk to your vet about the advisability of a veteran food and about any changes he or she might suggest in health care.

Living With a GSD

German Shepherd Dogs were developed to work in many different areas, from herding to police work. Their ability to reason made them ideal as guide dogs. Because of their keen intelligence and their dedication to their families, it's important to continue both socialisation and training for the life of the dog. They learn quickly, but because of their intelligence, they are also quick to consider what they think is a better, or faster, way to perform a task. Without continuous socialisation and training, they will make up their own rules, and those rules might not agree with those of the humans in the family. Without a firm leader, Shepherds are quite willing to take over the position.

German Shepherd Dogs are active dogs, and they need to have something to do to keep both their bodies and minds occupied. A casual stroll around the block morning and night is probably not going to be enough exercise for your Shepherd. If you jog, bicycle, have enough garden for a good game of fetch or Frisbee, or if you have children to keep your dog busy, that

With their own children, Shepherds are gentle, patient, and protective.

should do the trick. Besides physical activity, try to play games that will also keep your Shepherd's mind busy. Hide and seek is good, or you can hide treats and let your dog use his nose to find the goodies.

If you don't plan to include the dog as part of the family and don't want a dog living in the house, better pass on this breed. Shepherds bond strongly with their people, and they don't do well left on their own. This doesn't mean you can't ever leave your dog, but it does mean that when you are home, you need to include your GSD in your activities. If you're gone all day, leave a chew toy that holds food treats to give your dog something to do.

The Shepherd can adjust to apartment living, but you'll need to pay special attention to his exercise. Locate a dog park where he can run, or find someone with a compatible dog and organise play dates. Jog around the neighbourhood in early morning or evening when streets and parks may be less crowded. Your Shepherd can adapt to almost anything, as long as he's not ignored.

Other Pets

Properly introduced, Shepherds should live in harmony with other family dogs and with cats. One way to ease tension between dogs is to choose a dog of the opposite sex for the second family dog. Make introductions in a neutral area, and keep dogs on slack leads until you're sure they will get along. Feed animals separately to prevent arguments over dinner. If you have a cat or are getting one, make sure your

FAMILY-FRIENDLY TIP

German Shepherd Dogs and Children

No matter what the breed, children should always learn their "ABCs"—Ask Before Cuddling. This rule is especially important with large breeds like the German Shepherd Dog, which was bred to protect property and people. With their own children, Shepherds are gentle, patient, and protective. With children outside the family, use common sense. Make sure children are introduced to the dog with adult supervision.

Remember that the herding instinct may mean your dog will chase running children and nip their heels. If your Shepherd thinks one of "his" children is being threatened, he may take steps to end the threat. With a large group of strange children playing, if you can't actively supervise your dog, it may be best to separate the dog from the activity.

cat always has an escape route. Put a baby gate across a doorway so the cat can jump in or out, but the dog can't. Many Shepherds love and protect the family cat.

With smaller pets like gerbils or hamsters, it's better to be safe than sorry. Small, scurrying, squeaking animals trigger the prey drive, and while some dogs may cuddle up with the family guinea pig, it's more likely that the dog will consider the other animal lunch. Keep small pets safe in cages, and make sure your dog can't reach the cage.

The German Shepherd is a working dog with the build and the stamina to do whatever job he is given, and the intelligence and temperament for those jobs as well. It's a safe bet that your Shepherd will be able to join the family in any activity from jogging to football and anything in between. If you decide to compete in a performance event, your Shepherd will be ready, willing, and able.

German Shepherd Dogs

This GSD, Kenai, helps her owner take care of rescued cats.

Famous GSDs

In 1987, Ch. Covy Tucker Hill's Manhattan became the first German Shepherd Dog to win Best in Show at the Westminster Kennel Club Dog Show, the most prestigious dog show in the US. "Hatter" was shown by James Moses. He was bred by Cappy Pottle and Gloria Birch and owned by Shirlee Braunstein and Jane A. Firestone. Long before Hatter's win in the show ring, though, German Shepherd Dogs had captured hearts in the movies. Rin Tin Tin, Strongheart, and the Littlest Hobo (played by a dog named London) all captivated moviegoers in the twentieth century. More recently, All Dogs Go to Heaven featured a German Shepherd Dog named Charlie.

The most famous GSD is Rin Tin Tin, who started life in France, where a US soldier, Lee Duncan, found a litter of puppies in a bombed-out kennel. Duncan kept two of the puppies, naming the female, Nanette, and the male, Rin Tin Tin, after a small puppet given to soldiers by French children for good luck. (Nanette later died of distemper).

In 1922 Rin-Tin-Tin starred in The Man From Hell's River and went on to star in 26 Warner Brothers films. The dog's popularity is credited with saving Warner Brothers from bankruptcy.

Several of Rin Tin Tin's offspring also became performers, and while you may not see Rin Tin Tin on the silver screen anymore, his descendants are still going strong as working dogs. Duncan bred several litters of Shepherds, and in 1957, Jannettia Brodsgaard Propps acquired four of the Duncan-bred Shepherds, as well as his endorsement for her breeding programme.

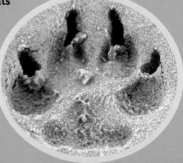

In 1988, the kennel passed to Ms. Propps' granddaughter, Daphne Hereford, who continues to breed German Shepherd Dogs that are direct descendants of Rin Tin Tin IV. The majority of puppies produced are placed with disabled children as assistance dogs through the A Rinty for Kids (ARFkids) Foundation.

Chapter 2

The Stuff of
Everyday Life

Your dog won't need his own DVD player or designer shoes, but there's still plenty of shopping you need to do. Your dog *will* need his own dishes, a place to sleep, a bed, a collar, a lead, and appropriate toys. It's great fun to go on a dog-based spending spree, but shop wisely. A toy that's too small, for instance can harm your dog. Think about your lifestyle and your German Shepherd Dog before you shop.

Take some time to think about what will work best in your home, and then dust off the credit card and start shopping!

Crate

At the top of your shopping list should be a crate. You may never have used a crate before and may think it looks like a jail. You may not like the idea of putting your adorable puppy in a confining box, but if that's what you think, you're thinking like a human. When it comes to crates, you have to think like a dog. Dogs like small, cozy, dark, safe places. Dogs don't think of crates as a prison but rather as a secure den. Many dogs will retreat to their crates for a nap on their own and will sleep in them at night, even with the door open. And, besides giving your dog his own spot, a crate makes housetraining much easier.

One word of warning: crate use can be abused. A crate is *not* a substitute for care. Use it for housetraining. Use it to keep your puppy safe when you're not home. Use it to keep your puppy from being underfoot, but don't just put your puppy in the crate and forget him. While there are the occasional exceptions, a good rule is to never leave your puppy or adult German Shepherd Dog crated for more than four hours.

What Type?

Crates come in many sizes. You can either purchase a smaller size for your puppy and then buy a larger one when he's an adult or, you can start with the adult size and make a barrier so that the crate is a good size for housetraining. If he can help it, your puppy won't want to soil his own bed. A crate that is too large gives him room to turn one end into a bedroom and the other end into a bathroom. A barrier will reduce the area and help keep him from toileting in the crate.

A crate will be a secure den for your GSD.

Crates come in solid plastic, wire, wood, and metal. Wood is very expensive and metal tends to hold in heat, so the best choices for home use are the solid plastic and the wire. There are advantages and disadvantages to both. A plastic crate is more den-like and private—the solid sides make your puppy feel more secure. The disadvantage is that it can hold in heat during the summer. A wire crate offers more ventilation and will usually have an easy-to-remove tray bottom for cleaning, but your dog may not find it as cozy and secure. If you choose a wire crate, cover it with a blanket or towels for a more private and secure place for your dog. In the summer, you can always flip back the blanket to allow more ventilation.

Spending money on a well-made crate is a good investment—while it may seem expensive, it will last the life of your dog.

Dog Bed

There are almost as many types of dog beds as there are toys, but the best bed for a young puppy may be a nest of old towels or an old flannel sheet. Even a well-trained puppy can have an accident, and old towels are absorbent and easy to wash. Some beds can take days to thoroughly dry. Also, puppies chew. It's not too upsetting when a puppy chews a hole in an old towel, but if your puppy destroys an expensive dog bed, you're not going to be happy.

If you buy a good bed now, it will either be too big, or your puppy will

The Importance of Schedules

Dogs are creatures of habit and do well with a structured routine. You'll find a suggested schedule for housetraining in Chapter 6, but even an adult dog will benefit from a schedule. Set times for feeding, walking, and playing to help your dog feel secure. Also, having a regular walk time helps your dog control his bladder.

outgrow it. Wait a while, and then invest. By the time your puppy has grown a bit, you'll know if he likes to curl up or stretch out when he sleeps. Some dogs like to have their heads on a pillow. If that's your dog, there are beds with raised edges. There are also beds that have small inner spring mattresses.

Whatever you choose for a bed, place it in a draught-free area. If your dog will be sleeping in his crate, he's already protected from draughts. Also, think about letting your dog sleep in a bedroom with a family member. Dogs, especially German Shepherds, love to be with their people. Letting them sleep in a bedroom gives them eight hours of time with you with no effort on your part.

You may even decide to let your dog sleep on the bed. That's your decision, but remember, that cute puppy will grow to a large adult. If you don't want 70 pounds (31.8 kg) of dog sleeping with you, don't let him sleep with you when he only weighs 20 pounds (9.1 kg). GSDs are smart, and if you give them an inch, they'll be more than happy to take the mile. It's much harder to break a habit than it is to never start it in the first place. Make a decision, stick to it, and be sure every member of the family sticks to it as well. It's confusing and unfair to the dog if one person allows him on a bed and another person yells at him for the same behaviour.

Ex-pen

While not an absolute necessity, an exercise pen, or ex-pen for short, is a handy item to have. Ex-pens are bottomless, topless wire pens that look a bit like a baby's playpen. They confine your dog to one small area and can be useful if you're housetraining your dog without using a crate. An ex-pen can contain your puppy in one section of the kitchen, family room, or porch. When you're travelling, an ex-pen is a safe way to contain your pet outside without tying him up.

Food and Water Bowls

You'll need food and water bowls for your pal. Stainless steel is an excellent choice for bowls, since it can be easily cleaned, won't break, and is lightweight. Many of the larger sizes also have a bit of rubber on the bottom to make them

Don't leave your GSD on the floor—get him a comfy bed!

A ceramic food bowl is hard for your GSD to tip over.

room, or keep him out. While he's being trained you may not want him in certain rooms, or you may want to have a "safe" room for the family cat. A baby gate allows you to block off rooms without closing doors.

Grooming Tools

As long as you're shopping, don't forget the basic grooming tools. You'll need nail clippers or a grinding tool, a comb,

non-skid. A ceramic dish may appeal to you because of a cute design or a bright colour, but if you decide on ceramic, make sure the glaze is lead-free. Ceramic makes a good, heavy dish that is hard to tip over, but it is also breakable.

Plastic is another choice and has the advantage of being both lightweight and non-breakable; but plastic is harder to thoroughly clean, and your dog may be able to easily tip it over. Plastic can also lead to a case of acne on your dog's chin.

Whatever kind of dishes you choose, make sure that they are always clean for your dog. The water dish should be emptied and rinsed at least once a day, and your dog should always have access to cool, clean water. Wash your dog's food dish, too. Most dogs will lick the bowl clean, but just because it looks clean doesn't mean it is clean. If you licked your dinner plate, it wouldn't really be clean, and neither is your dog's dish. Wash it between feedings, the same way you wash your dinner dishes.

Gate

Another handy item is a baby gate. Gates can keep your puppy in a particular

19

SENIOR DOG TIP

Helping an Older Dog Adapt

Puppies quickly adapt to their surroundings, but an older dog may need a little help. If you're giving a home to an older dog, try to stick to whatever schedule he may have been used to. If you know when he was fed and walked, try to follow that schedule for the first few weeks. If he's always been allowed to sleep on the couch, think about whether you can cover your couch and allow him that same privilege. Keep him on the same food he's always had. If you make a change, make it gradual.

The Stuff of Everyday Life

and a slicker brush. You may also want a shedding rake, a currycomb, and a good brush. Find out more about grooming your GSD in Chapter 4.

Identification

Another very important part of your shopping list is identification for your dog. It is almost impossible to think that you could ever lose your GSD, but accidents can happen. If your dog should get lost, he stands a reasonable chance of being returned to you safe and sound if he has some form of identification.

ID Tag

You can make up a tag with your name and phone number and attach it to your dog's collar. Tags come in different shapes and sizes. You can also get barrel-shaped discs where you write your contact details on a slip of paper inside the disc. Make sure you regularly check that the details on the disc are are easily readable.

Microchipping

For more permanent identification, talk to your vet about microchipping your pet. Microchips are tiny implants the size of a grain of rice. These are placed between the shoulder blades of your dog and are read by scanners. The chip contains a registration number, and by calling the chip

registry, a vet or rescue centre can get your contact information. Microchips are safe and permanent, and almost all vets and rescue centres have the scanners to read them.

Tattoos

If you purchased your puppy from a breeder, he may already be tattooed. If not, you may want to consider it. Typically, a tattoo of a number is placed on the inner thigh (the number is usually your puppy's registration number). Just remember that not

This police dog is clearly marked by the badge around his neck.

everyone knows enough to look for a tattoo. Also, as your dog grows, the tattoo can stretch and fade, or fur may cover the number.

Collar and Lead

Next on your shopping list should be a lead and collar. Your puppy will grow, so don't fall for that beautiful-looking expensive leather collar until he's full-grown. Instead, start with a flat, nylon buckle collar. Many of these are made so that the tongue of the buckle can be pushed through the collar at any point, so that the collar can expand with the dog. For an all-day, every-day collar, you'll want a flat, buckle collar of some type. Some trainers and show people use a chain training collar or a martingale collar, but those are best left to the professionals. If a training collar ring gets caught on something, it can choke your dog. Martingale collars have a second loop that runs through the ring ends on the actual collar. An unattended dog can get a foot, or even his lower jaw, caught on this loop and be seriously injured.

A harness is an alternative to a collar, but unless there's a medical reason why your dog needs a harness (if he's hurt his throat or had surgery on his neck) I don't recommend one. A harness limits your control over your dog and makes it very easy for your dog to pull.

Many stores have nylon leads that match the colour of the collars they sell, and it's fun to be colour-coordinated. The best length for a lead is six feet. Nylon leads are fine, and so are cotton or leather ones. Vinyl is not a great

FAMILY-FRIENDLY TIP

Kids as Caretakers

A dog can be a wonderful companion for a child, and having dog-related chores can teach a child responsibility; but a child should never be a dog's sole caretaker. Choose age-appropriate jobs for your child like changing the water in the water bowl or measuring the dog food. An older child may be able to walk or brush your German Shepherd Dog; but children can forget, and your dog shouldn't suffer because of it. It's up to you to make sure your dog is properly fed, watered, and exercised, no matter what your children do. Keeping yearly health care appointments and proper training is up to you—it may be "the kids' dog" but he is ultimately your responsibility.

choice because it won't last and is not as flexible as the other types. Stay away from chain leads. You might think that a chain lead connotes "strength," and while it might, it is not very useful. When you are walking a dog, you should have one hand on the loop at the end, and the other about half way down the lead. If you do that with a chain and your dog makes a sudden lunge for a

Hiring Help

German Shepherd puppies have lots of bounce and lots of energy. Hiring a dog walker or a dog sitter a few times a week can help your puppy burn off excess energy and may prevent destructive behaviour at home. This is particularly important if you have to go out to work. An adult dog should not be left for longer than four hours. There may be a neighbour you can rely on to help out. If you decide on a neighbour to walk your dog, make sure it is someone who can control your dog in public.

rabbit, that chain will tear the skin on your hand.

Another kind of lead is the retractable kind that comes in 15 and 25-foot (4.6 and 7.6 m) lengths. These are fine for giving your dog exercise in an open area, but they are not good for a walk around the block. They can give a dog too much freedom and are harder to use when you want to keep your dog by your side as you pass other people or dogs on your walk.

Toys

Toys are the fun part of the shopping list. There are dozens of wonderful toys out there, so you're only limited by your budget. There

A nylon collar is a good choice for your puppy.

are two things to think about when you buy a toy. The first is: is it big enough? A ball that is just right for a terrier will be too small for your German Shepherd Dog. A toy that may be too big is better than one that is too small. A small toy can get caught in your dog's throat, or if swallowed whole, can block his intestine and require surgery.

The second thing to think about is: can your dog chew off pieces and swallow them? This may require trial and error. Some dogs can be given a stuffed toy, and they will carry it around and never tear or rip it. Other dogs will immediately tear the toy open, exposing stuffing and the hidden noisemaker inside. My female dog is content to carry around her stuffed bear and only occasionally bite it. My male can destroy a stuffed toy in about ten minutes—he concentrates on the area where the squeaker is and rips a hole. If I didn't supervise his play, he would probably swallow the plastic noisemaker, as well as mouthfuls of the stuffing. It's fun to watch him with a toy, but the minute he tears it apart, I take it away. His play is always supervised.

My male also destroys latex squeaky toys, so I cut out the part that makes the toy squeak before I give it to him. While I also supervise these toys to make sure he doesn't swallow large chunks of the latex, don't worry if your dog swallows a few tiny bits. The latex will pass harmlessly through your dog's system.

If your dog is teething, he may enjoy a hard rubber toy, and many of these also have a hole that will hold cheese or peanut butter, giving your dog something to do when he's left alone.

Toys don't have to be fancy, either. Some dogs enjoy playing with a milk carton, and a carrot can make a wonderful chew stick for a puppy. Just remember to supervise play if your dog enjoys playing with a milk carton. You don't want him gnawing it to pieces.

23

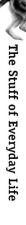

The Stuff of Everyday Life

The Expert Knows

Exercise!

All dogs need a certain amount of exercise, but with an active, intelligent breed like the German Shepherd Dog, it's especially important. Large dogs need exercise for muscle development and tone, and exercise will tire your dog out, making him easier to live with indoors. Playing games will give your GSD a chance to use that brain of his in an acceptable activity, instead of thinking up games like "shred the pillow" or "dig under the fence."

Chapter 3

Good Eating

Dogs, like people, need a balanced diet to stay healthy. They need water and food, and the food they eat must include protein, fat, carbohydrates, vitamins, and minerals. They also need food especially formulated for dogs. A diet that works for a person is probably not the best diet for a dog. The dog "food pyramid" is heavier in proteins and fats than in carbohydrates. And, some foods that we enjoy can harm our dogs. Chocolate can be deadly, onions can cause a form of anaemia, and Macadamia nuts can cause temporary paralysis. Feed your dog like a dog, no matter how much he pleads for a share of your dinner.

Your dog needs a diet with the right balance of protein and fat.

26

Commercial Diets

At one time, dogs were fed whatever was left over from the family table and may not have always had a balanced diet. Today, commercial dog food companies have made it easy to feed our dogs what they need. Every supermarket has shelves full of nutritionally balanced foods. This doesn't mean that every food is right for every dog. Dogs can develop food allergies, just like people. Some foods may be too rich for one dog and just right for another. A very active dog will need a different diet from a dog that just gets moderate exercise.

You have several choices when it comes to commercial food.

Canned Food

Canned foods are more expensive than dry foods and must be refrigerated after opening. Like dry food, they should contain a major protein source and will have added vitamins and minerals. There may or may not be a grain ingredient. They have more water in them than other types of commercial foods but have the advantage of smelling great (at least to your dog, if not to you). A picky eater may be more apt to eat canned than dry; some owners mix canned and dry together to stretch their budgets and tempt their dogs. Canned food also offers a good place to hide medicine if you ever have to dose your GSD.

Dry Food

Dry food is the least expensive dog food on the market. The texture gives your dog the benefit of chewing, which may help keep his teeth clean. Dry food contains a protein source like beef, chicken, turkey, or lamb, and a filler grain. Corn is commonly used, but the grain may also be wheat, rice, or soya. There will be added vitamins and a preservative. Dry food doesn't need refrigeration, but it can get stale, or depending on the fat content, turn rancid. Buy dry food in the smallest size bag possible to help keep it fresh. If your dog takes more than three or four weeks to eat a bag, you need to buy a smaller bag. There are also storage bins you can buy that have air-tight lids to help keep food fresh.

Semi-moist Food

Semi-moist food is the most expensive food you can buy your GSD. It is frequently moulded into shapes that remind people of fresh meat, meat patties, or bits of cheese. These foods are convenient—and most dogs love them—but they typically contain more sugar and flour than either dry or canned foods. Those are the ingredients that keep the food soft. Semi-moist foods have more food colouring in them than the other types of commercial food. Neither sugar nor refined flour adds any nutritional value to the food, and your dog doesn't need extra sugar any more than you do. Sugar is also bad for teeth, and although most dogs gulp food so quickly there's not a lot of contact with the teeth, semi-moist bits of food can adhere to teeth surfaces and could, long term, harm teeth.

Reading Food Labels

Whether you choose a dry, canned, or semi-moist food,

Table Manners

Your dog won't be eating at the table with you, but that doesn't mean he shouldn't be taught manners. You may think it's cute when your little German Shepherd puppy begs or jumps up for the food in your hand, but it isn't as cute when it's a 75-pound (35 kg) adult. It's harder to break a habit than it is to start it, so the family rule should be no feeding the dog from the table.

Good manners for your dog should include waiting until you put down the food dish. A dog should sit or stand in place until the dish is on the floor, and you have given permission for him to eat. The same goes for any treats. Ask your dog to sit or lie down before you give him anything edible.

unnecessary—and empty—calories.

there should be a label giving an analysis of the contents. In the UK, there are guidelines on labels laid down by the Food Standards Agency (FSA), which controls the pet food industry. The FSA has to conform to EC guidelines.

Animal-based protein should be one of the first five ingredients listed on the label, and ideally, should be one of the first three ingredients. Don't be put off by the phrase "animal by-products." This includes organ meats and can provide valuable nutrients to your dog.

The label will list preservatives, if any. Many people prefer a food with a natural preservative, like vitamin E, which doesn't last quite as long as synthetic preservatives. Keep in mind the label will only list what preservatives, if any, the manufacturer added. There's no way to know what preservatives might already be in the ingredients used to make the food. Buy smaller quantities of naturally preserved food to ensure freshness.

One last thing is to check the label for added sugars. The label may say sugar, corn syrup, or sucrose. These are

What's Best for My GSD?

What type of food you choose for your German Shepherd Dog will depend on what your dog likes to eat and what works the best at keeping him healthy. It may take some trial and error to find the best food. Generally, top of the line, brand-name foods are your best choice, but the only way to know if you've made the right food choice is to look at your dog. Your dog's coat should be shiny and thick. He should have energy and bright, clear eyes. His stools should be firm, and he shouldn't be vomiting. If your dog is biting or licking at his paws, if his coat is dry and dull, or if he has diarrhoea or is vomiting, it could be his food.

Have your vet rule out any physical problems and then check the label on your dog food. If corn is the main grain used, try switching to a food that uses rice or wheat. If the main protein is beef, try chicken or lamb. Another problem may be that the food is too rich for your dog. Try a food with a lower level of protein or fat. If these changes don't help, you may need to try a one-ingredient food (usually available from your vet), and then start the slow process of determining just what ingredient is causing the problem. If you do decide to switch the food your dog is eating, gradually replace the old with the new over a period of about five days, to prevent diarrhoea or vomiting.

Non-commercial Options

All commercial foods have the advantage of being quick and easy, but some people want more control over what their dog is eating. Cooking for your dog or feeding a raw diet can be the answer. Both of these methods take more time than feeding commercial foods, and both require attention to balancing the diet. Feeding a raw diet does not mean your dog just eats meat and bones, and cooking doesn't mean feeding your GSD table scraps.

Raw Diet

The raw diet is commonly called the BARF diet, which stands for Bones and Raw Food or Biologically Appropriate Raw Food. With this diet, a dog is fed raw, meaty bones (chicken necks and backs are a frequent choice), organ meat, muscle meat, and vegetables.

FAMILY-FRIENDLY TIP

Helping Hands

Children enjoy helping to feed the family dog, and with supervision, even a very young child can help put food in a bowl and place the bowl on the floor. If you have an adult dog, tell the dog to "stay" or hold the dog until the child sets the bowl down. A German Shepherd Dog can easily knock a child over on his way to dinner. Make sure the child never teases the dog, holding the food over his head, or starting to give the food to the dog and then withdrawing it. Food is not a toy. Make sure the child understands that the dog must be left alone while he is eating. There should be no hugging, petting, or tugging. Let the dog eat quietly.

The raw diet is not without controversy. Some vets are against feeding raw meat because of the health threat of salmonella and *E. coli* in raw foods; others say that the benefits outweigh the possible danger. People who feed raw claim shinier coats, cleaner teeth, and fewer health problems for their dogs. Do

If you have the time, you might want to try home-cooking for your GSD.

SENIOR DOG TIP

Feeding the Older Dog

As your dog ages, you may need to adjust how and what you feed him. As he becomes less active, he'll need fewer calories and less protein. It might be time for a senior food. He may develop an ailment that requires a special diet. Cracked or broken teeth may cause pain and prevent your dog from eating. A special senior checkup from your vet, complete with blood tests, will help you decide what changes in diet you might need to make to keep your dog happy and healthy as he gets older.

your research and talk to your vet if you think the raw diet is right for your German Shepherd Dog.

In her book, *Switching to Raw*, Susan K. Johnson gives suggested quantities for an eighty-pound dog. Six or seven chicken wings, one or two large turkey necks, or four chicken backs would make a raw, meaty bone meal. You can grind the bones for puppies until they are able to crunch them up themselves, and if the idea of bones still bothers you, continue to grind them for your adult.

For a vegetable meal, Johnson suggests one and a half cups of vegetable mix, a can of fish, and a couple of eggs. Vegetables must be broken down in a blender or a food processor because dogs can't break down the cellulose in plants. Almost any vegetable that your dog will eat may be added to the vegetable mix. Never include onions, which can cause haemolytic anaemia in dogs.

Muscle and organ meat meals would be about three quarters of a pound of meat. Many dogs also love tripe, which is an animal's stomach lining and can be bought fresh or frozen. Many people who feed raw also give their dogs a multi-vitamin daily.

If you decide to feed raw, you'll need enough freezer space to store all the meat and bones that your dog will need. A large freezer also means you can take advantage of sales. Most people who feed raw make up large batches of vegetable mix and freeze individual meal portions, so you'll need the freezer space for that, too.

Home-cooked Diet

You may decide that you don't want to feed your German Shepherd Dog a raw diet because of concerns over bacteria, but you would like to give your dog fresher foods than commercial products. Cooking for your dog may be the right choice for you.

As with the raw diet, you need to give your dog a balanced diet of vitamins, minerals, proteins, fats, and carbohydrates. A cooked vegetable mixture with the addition of oatmeal makes a good base for a non-meat meal. You can then add the same types of meats as in the raw diet, only cooked. Cook ground beef or turkey, liver, and chicken gizzards. The one thing you must never, ever give your dog, though, is cooked bones. Raw bones are softer and can be chewed up and swallowed. Cooked bones, of any kind, can splinter and puncture your dog's intestines. Cooked bones are also harder than raw and can result in cracked or broken teeth.

If you want your dog to get the benefit of bones (calcium), you can cook chicken legs in a crock-pot. Cover the chicken with water and cook on low for 24 hours. This turns the bones to mush so they're safe for your dog to eat.

Most people who cook for their dogs prepare the food in bulk and then freeze individual portions. If you decide to cook for your German Shepherd Dog, talk to your veterinary surgeon

Proponents of non-commercial diets say their dogs are healthier and full of energy.

Supplements

If you are feeding your dog a balanced diet, and he is healthy, you shouldn't need to add any supplements. If your dog has a health problem, your vet may prescribe a specific supplement to help your dog. For instance, a dog with a kidney ailment may be helped by a supplement of B vitamins. German Shepherd Dogs, as a breed, are susceptible to inflammatory bowel disease, an illness that prevents proper absorption of B vitamins. A vet will frequently prescribe a vitamin B complex.

about the advisability of adding a vitamin supplement.

Variety Is the Spice of Life

If you feed a commercial food, and your dog does well on it (i.e., he's healthy and there are no sign of allergies), you might be inclined to never change his food. However, there is a school of thought that says no matter what you feed your dog, there should be variety; dogs shouldn't eat the same food day in and day out.

If you feed one food constantly, your dog's body won't be able to handle food it's not used to. That is one of the reasons why a food change for your dog should be done gradually over a week or so. It's the same principle for vegetarians who will get physically ill if they eat meat. That's because their system hasn't experienced meat in so long that it can't handle it.

Vet Wendy Blount notes, "I have German Shepherds, a breed notorious for their sensitive GI tracts. Every time I open a new bag of dog food, it's a different brand/flavour than the last. And every night I open a can of food that is different than the night before. They get a variety of fresh foods as a 'top dressing.' I have a list of several dozen varieties of dry food and canned foods I rotate through—all whole foods with no chemical preservatives (that I know of)."

I have a dog with food allergies, and it took me so long to finally find a food he could tolerate that, even though I think variety is a good idea, and I understand the benefits of fresher foods, I continue to feed the commercial brand that helps him stay healthy.

Talk to breeders, your vet, and other dog owners about their choice of doggy diet. Feed your GSD what you feel comfortable with, as long as it keeps him healthy. If you don't have the time to feed raw or home-cook properly, it's better to stick with a commercial food. You won't be doing

Feeding Chart

This chart is only a general guideline for feeding your German Shepherd Dog. Follow suggestions from your breeder and your vet. Your dog may need more or less food than another dog of the same breed or more or less food depending on the brand you choose. With large dogs like German Shepherds, some breeders recommend using adult food even for puppies to prevent joint stress from too rapid growth. A senior dog may do just fine on the adult food he's always eaten.

Sample Feeding Schedule for Each Phase of Your GSD's Life

Age	Times per Day	Amount	Best Food
Puppies (up to 6 months)	2-3 depending on age	275ml - 410ml each feeding	Puppy food
Adolescents (6 months to 18 months)	2	550ml - 825ml each feeding	Adult food
Active Adult (18 years to 7 years)	1 or 2	825ml - 1100ml total	Adult/active food
Sedentary Adults (7 to 9 years)	1 or 2	825ml - 1100ml total	Adult or senior food
Seniors (9 plus years)	2	825ml total	Adult or senior food

Puppies should be fed 2 or 3 times a day.

the risk of spoiled food full of bacteria. If you have two or more dogs, and you free feed, there's no way of knowing how much food each dog is getting. A stronger, more dominant dog may be getting the majority of the food, leaving a more timid dog with less than he needs.

Another disadvantage of free feeding is those times you need to medicate your dog. Many medications need to be given at a specific time, with food. A dog used to nibbling at his food all day long may not get the full dose of a liquid or powder at the proper time.

your German Shepherd Dog any good if you cut corners.

Free Feeding or Scheduled Feeding?

Some people measure out their dog's food and then leave the food available all day for the dog to nibble at whenever he's hungry. That method of feeding is called "free feeding." Other owners schedule meals at a regular time and pick up the dish after 15 or 20 minutes.

If you only have one dog, and you feed a dry, commercial food, free feeding may work well for you. If you feed canned food, a raw diet, or you cook for your dog, free feeding is not a good idea—it invites bugs, flies, and

Obesity

Obesity is just as bad for dogs as it is for people. It can lead to joint stress, heart problems, and diabetes. Most often, obese dogs are the product of too much food and too little exercise. It's easy to equate love with food when it comes to our dogs. They are so good at looking cute and pathetic that it's hard to resist giving them part of a sandwich or an extra dog biscuit—that happy tail wagging can make us forget about the extra calories in the treat. Fortunately, you can control what your dog eats. If you notice your GSD looking a bit pudgy, you can reduce the amount of food. After all, dogs can't open the refrigerator and sneak a midnight snack or raid the freezer for a scoop of ice cream.

A dog at the right weight shows a slight indentation behind the ribs when you look down on the dog. Run your hands over your dog's sides. You should be able to feel the ribs. If you can count the ribs or if your dog's back bone shows, he is underweight. If you can't feel the ribs, and there's no clear indentation behind the ribs, your dog needs to go on a diet. If weight gain or loss is sudden, or given the amount of food you're feeding, you don't feel there should be a gain or loss, check with your veterinary surgeon for other problems that may cause these symptoms.

Dogs are creatures of habit. If you always give your dog a biscuit when he comes in the house, he'll always expect one. To help cut it down, break

You can avoid obesity in your GSD by controlling his diet and giving him plenty of exercise.

Treats

Treats are all the extra goodies your German Shepherd Dog gets that are not part of his regular meals. A treat can be a bit of gravy on his kibble or a spoonful of mashed potato. A treat can be a dog biscuit or the final bite of your turkey sandwich. You may be using treats to train your dog in obedience or agility. Treats have their place, but they can also be overdone. Treats should make up no more than 10 percent of your dog's total diet. If you use treats for training, cut up soft treats into teeny, tiny pieces. Your dog will work for those small pieces just as enthusiastically as for large chunks. If your dog enjoys dog cookies, break them in half. Limit table scraps to the occasional treat.

the treat in half—he'll be happy, and you'll save a few calories. Your dog may notice that his food dish is not quite as full as usual, and he may look around

for more to eat. Adding green beans won't add much in the way of calories but will help to fill your dog up. You can ask your vet for additional foods that you can use to add bulk without adding fat and calories.

A little more exercise will help your dog reduce his weight as well. Add another walk to his day, or go a few more times around the block. Play with a ball or Frisbee in the garden. If your dog has a canine friend, arrange a couple of play dates each week. Any or all of these, combined with smaller meals, will soon have your dog back to his correct weight.

Foods to Avoid

A dog will eat just about anything, so it's up to you to make sure your dog doesn't eat the wrong things. Following is a list of foods and other ingestible items to avoid giving your dog:

- Products sweetened with Xylitol, an artificial sweetener, may be toxic to dogs.

- Chocolate contains theobromine, which is toxic to dogs. Just three ounces of baking chocolate can kill a medium-sized dog. Milk chocolate is less dangerous, but if your dog eats enough of it, it can make him very sick or even kill him. Take special care around the holidays, and keep chocolate treats away from your dog.

- Large amounts of grapes or raisins have been implicated in acute kidney failure in dogs. You don't need to panic if your dog eats a few raisins or a grape, but if your dog finds an entire box of raisins and thinks it is a wonderful snack, check in with your vet.

- Onions can induce haemolytic anaemia in dogs.

- Raw egg whites contain a protein called avidin, which binds up biotin, a B vitamin, making it impossible for a dog to use the biotin. Cooking the egg white changes the character of the avidin so it can no longer bind to the biotin.

- Too many macadamia nuts can cause temporary paralysis of the hindquarters. The paralysis will wear off, but it's frightening when it happens.

- Coffee and tea may perk you up, but both these beverages contain caffeine and theobromine, so they're on your dog's "can't have" list.

- It's okay to give him a buffered aspirin if he's pulled a muscle or seems stiff and sore, but stay away from paracetamol.

- You'll know enough not to let your dog ingest cleaning products, but remember, anti-freeze is deadly as well. Anti-freeze tastes sweet, so dogs love it: but just a small amount will kill your dog. If you suspect your dog has swallowed anti-freeze, get him to your vet without delay.

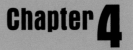
Looking Good

German Shepherd Dogs don't need fancy grooming. Unlike a Poodle or a Bichon Frise, who need professional care, you can groom your German Shepherd yourself without much effort. However, grooming isn't just about getting rid of dead hair and cleaning teeth. Grooming also offers a chance for you to bond with your dog.

W hen you're grooming, all of your attention is focused on your dog. There should be no interruptions during the sessions. You can take the time to talk to your dog and give him special treats when he's being good. Give him a massage if he enjoys that, and make grooming a special time for just the two of you.

Brushing

GSDs have a thick double coat: a soft fluffy undercoat to keep the dog warm, and a longer, harsher outer coat to shed rain and snow and repel dirt. Your Shepherd will shed year round, but twice a year he'll get rid of that fluffy undercoat. This is known as "blowing coat," and this is the time you'll really need to keep up with his brushing—either every day or every other day to help you control the shed and keep your GSD looking good. The rest of the year, a good brushing once or twice a week will be enough.

Unlike some other breeds with longer coats, there's not much danger of mats forming on your Shepherd. So if you miss a week of brushing, you may have more hair on your rug or on the furniture, but there won't be any painful mats to comb out.

Brushing not only gets rid of the dead, dry hair, it stimulates the skin and distributes the oils in the hair evenly. If you have a grooming table, that can make grooming easier because you won't have to bend over or kneel. I sometimes put a sheet over my bedspread and groom dogs on the bed. They're more willing to lie down, and I can do one side and then coax them to lie on the other side. Sometimes, with a

Use a shedding rake on your dog's coat when your GSD is shedding heavily.

Grooming Supplies

Grooming supplies you'll need for your GSD include:

- Nail clippers and/or a grinding tool. You'll find both of these items at your local pet supply store.
- Toothbrush and doggy toothpaste. Your vet will have these, or check your pet supply store.
- Ear cleaner. Your vet may sell a product, or you can buy it at your local pet supply store.
- Slicker brush. A slicker brush has wire bristles set at an angle. They work well at getting out heavy undercoat.
- Comb. Combs for dogs are just like combs for people—they straighten the hair after a good brushing and may also help remove undercoat.
- Flea comb. A flea comb is a very fine-toothed comb that traps fleas as you comb your dog.
- Shedding rake. Shedding rakes may be metal or rubber. They will get rid of more undercoat faster than a regular brush. A shedding rake can come in handy when your Shepherd is seriously shedding.
- Curry comb. A curry comb has short rubber nubs and helps loosen and remove dead outer coat.

Shepherd, you can just sit on the floor and groom. Whatever works best for you and your dog.

Start by spraying the coat with a bit of water. This helps stop static electricity from building up and prevents the coat from breaking. If your dog is shedding heavily, start with your shedding rake. Work from the neck to the tail in the direction that the fur grows. For normal brushing, start near the tail. Push fur back against the grain, and then use the slicker brush and briskly brush the fur away from your hand and back into place. When you've got out as much loose undercoat as you can, finish by combing in the direction of the fur from the neck to the tail.

Be gentle when you work on the tail so your brushing doesn't pull. You might want to use just a comb. Use it as you'd use the slicker brush.

Generally, your dog's head won't need much grooming. Wipe off his face with a damp cloth, check his ears, and you should be fine.

Bathing

If you brush your dog regularly, he shouldn't need frequent baths unless he gets extremely dirty or rolls in something undesirable. A dog who spends a lot of time outdoors will need more baths than a mostly indoor dog. Four baths a year should be fine unless you're treating a skin condition, and your vet prescribes baths more often.

Your own bath will work well for a bath, but wherever you decide to bathe your dog, remember to supply

Looking Good

a non-skid mat to prevent your dog from slipping and falling. Gather up all your supplies, including shampoo, cotton-wool balls, and a washcloth, and get them in the bathroom before you add the dog. You'll also need three or four big towels to dry your dog and a couple more for you to kneel on.

Once you have all of your supplies ready, go get your dog. Most dogs try to avoid baths; so don't use the "come" command for something he dislikes. Put his lead on if you have to, and give him a treat to thank him for following you nicely. Once you get the dog in the bathroom, shut the door. You don't want your dog escaping and spreading soap and water throughout the house.

Get the water to the right temperature—lukewarm—before you put the dog in the bath. It will be easier than trying to hold on to your GSD and adjusting the water at the same time: and it will prevent too hot water from burning your dog's toes. You can buy a special attachment for your tap that acts as a showerhead for your dog, or you can use a small pan or unbreakable jug to get your dog wet. Always use a shampoo made for dogs. People shampoo can dry out your dog's hair and skin. Be careful not to get soap into your dog's eyes. The best approach is to wipe off the face gently with a wet cloth, and only apply soap from the neck back. This also helps keep water

Daily brushing during heavy sheds will help cut down on the hair you find in your house.

from getting in your dog's ears. You can put a cotton-wool ball in each ear to keep the water out, but most dogs will just keep shaking their heads until they dislodge the cotton-wool.

Wet your dog all over and then work in the shampoo. Rinse him off and then shampoo him again. After the second lather, rinse thoroughly paying special attention to behind the elbows and the stomach. Soap that doesn't get rinsed away can cause itching and red skin. Rinse his feet thoroughly as well.

Grooming Tables

Grooming tables are dog-sized folding tables that have a non-skid surface and put your dog within easy reach for grooming. A table can really save your back, and a dog on a table may be less likely to wriggle and try to get away. You can also buy a grooming arm, shaped like an inverted "L," which extends over the table. You can fasten a loop to the arm and then slip the loop over your dog's head. This keeps his head up and out of your way, which is helpful when you're clipping nails.

Never, ever leave a dog unattended on a grooming table. If you're using a grooming loop, your dog could hang himself. If he's loose on the table, he could injure himself jumping off.

Drying
If you can keep your dog in the bath for a minute or two while he shakes, fine. Otherwise, try to get those towels wrapped around him quickly. You'd be amazed how much water a dog can shake out of his fur…and how wet it can make you. Towel off as much of the water as you can. If you're bathing your dog in the summer, he can air dry. If it's cold out, use a dryer. If you have dryer made especially for dogs, great. If you plan to use your human hair dryer, make sure you put it on the air only setting or at least on the lowest setting possible. A dog's skin is very sensitive, and you risk burning your dog if you use a higher setting. Keeping the dryer moving will also help prevent burns.

In cold weather, don't let your German Shepherd Dog out until he's thoroughly dry. This can take a long time with that thick undercoat, so make sure to give him a toilet break before the bath. In good weather, it's okay to let him out before he's dry, but don't be surprised if he immediately rolls on the ground. Just hope he rolls on grass and not in a patch of dirt!

Don't Forget the Collar
While you're waiting for your dog to dry, there's something else you should be cleaning—your dog's collar. It's easy to overlook the collar, but just like a person's shirt or blouse, that collar gets dirty with skin oils and

Grooming as a Health Check

One advantage to regular grooming is that you may find a health problem while it's still small. When you're grooming your dog, you're running your hands over his entire body. If he's got a lump or bump, you'll find it. Likewise, if he jerks or pulls away, this may mean he's got a bruise or sore that hurts when you touch it. Handling his feet gives you a chance to discover any cuts or scrapes on the pads or any growths between the toes.

Grooming also gives you a chance to check for fleas or ticks. During flea season, use the flea comb, or check your dog's stomach where the fur is thinner, especially toward the hind legs. You may see a flea or two scurrying for cover, or you may see the dark flecks of "flea dirt."

While you're grooming, check the inside of the ears for any sores or redness, and look at your dog's teeth. A build-up of plaque may mean you need to make an appointment for a professional teeth cleaning.

grime from your dog's fur. If you have a nylon collar, squirt on a bit of shampoo and scrub it with an old toothbrush. If the collar is leather, use saddle soap. Make sure the collar is completely dry before you put it back on your dog.

Ear Care

Once a month or so, use a squirt of ear cleaner and some cotton-wool balls to clean your dog's ears. Shepherds aren't prone to ear infections because those lovely, upright ears allow air to circulate; but dirt and wax can accumulate, so it's a good idea to clean the ears now and then. Never poke or push anything into the ear canal. Clean only as far as you can easily reach.

Even though Shepherds aren't prone to ear infections, that doesn't mean they might not get one. If your dog tips his head to one side, carries the ear lower than normal, scratches his ear, or rubs his head on the ground, make an appointment with your vet.

Eye Care

Your dog's eyes should be clear and bright with no discharge. If your dog is blinking, squinting, or is rubbing his eyes with his paw, make an appointment with your vet.

Nail Care

Keep your dog's nails trimmed. Short, tidy nails lessen the chance that family members will get scratched, and your GSD can walk better with short nails. Long nails also cause the foot to spread, separating the toes. Really long nails can make it very difficult for your dog to walk. If you take long walks with your dog on pavement, the nails may get worn down, but otherwise you'll need to trim them.

Nails grow at different rates on individual dogs. Some dogs need a quick trim once a week, others may be able to go for a month before they need those nails snipped. Check your dog's paws weekly, and trim or make an appointment with a groomer when needed.

Start trimming your dog's nails when he's just a puppy. Handle his feet several times a day so that he's used to someone picking up his feet. If your dog fusses when you try to cut his nails, do just one foot at a time, then stop and give your dog a treat. A bit later, do the nails on another foot, and so on, until the job is done.

There are two types of clippers. One is like a giant pair of scissors. The other, the guillotine, slices the nail. Use whichever you are comfortable with. Your dog can be standing, sitting, or lying down, whichever is the most comfortable for both of you. Grasp the paw firmly. If your dog is standing or sitting, you can use your shoulder to keep his nose out of the way. Trim the sharp tips of the nails being careful not to cut the quick. The quick is a small vein that runs through the middle of the nail and will bleed if cut. If your dog has white nails, you can see the quick. If your dog has black nails, you'll need to guess: so trim off just a little bit at a time. The quick usually stops just before the sharp hook at the end of the nail.

If you do hit the quick with the clippers, a dab of styptic powder will stop the bleeding. You'll find styptic powder at your pet supply store or the chemist. Hitting the quick hurts and your dog may yelp, but it's not life threatening.

It's important to keep your dog's nails trimmed.

FAMILY-FRIENDLY TIP

Children and Grooming

With the possible exceptions of ear cleaning and nail trimming, an older child can groom a German Shepherd Dog. Show the child how to use the curry comb, shedding rake, or the slicker brush. Make sure they understand that they shouldn't pull on or tug at the hair. Caution them to be gentle on the legs and not to do anything that seems to annoy or hurt the dog. Older teens should be able to clip nails and clean out the ears as well. Very young children may not be able to actually groom, but they can be given a soft bristle brush, and with supervision, can brush the dog. Emphasise the need to be gentle and the importance of stopping if the dog indicates that anything is hurting him.

Nail Grinders

Some dogs just hate having their nails cut, no matter how often you handle their feet, and no matter how gentle you are. For these dogs, you might want to try a nail grinder. Most dogs don't object to a grinder, which has an abrasive wheel at the tip that grinds away the nail. Get your dog used to the grinder by turning it on and holding the handle near his foot. Let him get used to the noise and the vibration. This may take several days. When he calmly accepts the grinder, you can start grinding his nails. As with the clippers, you may need to do just one foot at a time. Use lots of treats and lots of patience—don't turn nail time into a wrestling match.

Trimming

After you've trimmed your dog's nails, trim the fur on the bottom of his foot as well. Too much fur between the toes lessens your dog's traction, and it can trap snow and ice, making it hard for your dog to walk. Excess fur traps dirt, too, which means more dirt in your home as your dog goes in and out.

Dental Care

Your dog's teeth need attention, too. Dogs don't get cavities the way people do, but plaque can build up and serious infections can result. Brushing your dog's teeth is another part of keeping him healthy.

If you have a puppy, start getting him used to brushing right away. Older dogs may need a little more time and patience, but don't give up. Wrap your finger in a piece of gauze, then rub your finger over his teeth and gums. Do just a quarter of his mouth, then stop and give him a treat. Be gentle and don't force the issue. Rubbing a bit of meat on your finger may make him more willing to let you work on his mouth.

After your GSD accepts your finger on his teeth, you move on to

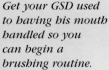

> Get your GSD used to having his mouth handled so you can begin a brushing routine.

using a toothbrush. There are actual toothbrushes made for dogs, and there are also rubber fingertip brushes that have a rough surface for brushing teeth. Toothpaste may make the job easier, but make sure it's a toothpaste for dogs. Human toothpaste can be harmful to your dog, and besides, toothpaste for people doesn't usually come in flavours like chicken or liver.

Get your dog used to the toothbrush or finger brush the same way you got him used to the gauze. Three times a week is a good schedule for brushing, but if you can't manage that, even once a week should slow the build up of tartar and plaque.

Groomers

With any of these grooming chores—ears, teeth, nails—if you aren't comfortable doing it yourself, take your dog to a groomer. The same goes for baths and brushing. If there's any reason at all why you can't do it yourself, make an appointment with a groomer. Grooming your German Shepherd Dog should never be neglected; after all, your dog's health is your responsibility.

Accessories

People with Poodles sometimes paint the dog's toenails, and for Shih Tzus, Yorkshire Terriers, and Maltese add a little flair, but otherwise he's fine the way he is.

The same goes for coats and sweaters. Some shorthaired dogs benefit from an extra bit of warmth on a cold winter's day, but your German Shepherd Dog has an all-weather coat of his own and doesn't need anything extra. If you're planning a long hike or a walk over sharp ice, booties may be a good idea; most other times your Shepherd can go barefoot with no problems at all.

German Shepherd Dogs

SENIOR DOG TIP

Grooming the Older Dog

Older dogs are apt to have odd lumps or bumps, such as benign fatty tumours, so be careful not to touch these while you're grooming. An older dog may also have arthritis and may not be able to stand for an extended period of time. Try to do as much as you can with your dog sitting or lying down. That same arthritis may make him sensitive to touch, so be gentle. The vigorous brushing you could give your young dog may be too much for an older dog. Break up grooming chores into short sessions—trim your senior's nails, and then wait for another day to brush his coat. If you can only do one side of your dog before he tires, then just do that.

grooming isn't complete without tiny bows—but your German Shepherd Dog doesn't need anything extra to make him look good. He won't mind wearing a bandana if you want to

A sporty bandanna might look great on your GSD.

You'll be amazed at all the hair you comb out of your German Shepherd Dog. You might even think that it would be fun to do something with all that hair. One thing you can do is spin it into yarn and knit a hat, a scarf, or a sweater.

The rule of thumb is that fur is spin-able if you can twist a small amount together and make a four to six inch piece of yarn that won't easily come apart when you pull on the ends. If it's too short, you won't be able to spin it by itself, but you can mix that fur with other types of fur or hair. Sheep's wool, Angora goat, or rabbit will all work. Even if you have fur that is long enough, dog hair doesn't have the lanolin or barbs that wool has, which helps it hold together.

Dog hair is very warm, but a word of warning: if dog hair is not cleaned properly after carding and spinning, it can smell like wet dog when it gets damp. No matter how beautiful the garment, you won't want to smell like a dog who's just come in from the rain.

If you do decide to try spinning, remember that the hair you want is the thick undercoat. The outer coat does not spin well at all. It's much too harsh and slippery. And use hair that is brushed out, not clipped. Clipped fur sheds after it is spun. Keep that in mind if you're blending your Shepherd's under coat with another animal's like rabbit.

If you think spinning and knitting with dog fur sounds like fun, read *Knitting with Dog Hair*, by Kendall Crolius and Anne Montgomery.

If you don't want to tackle the spinning project by yourself, see if there's a spinner in your area that might like the challenge or look in the classified ads of dog magazines. Many of them will spin your collected fur into a garment of your choice.

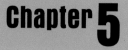

Chapter 5

Feeling Good

On the whole, German Shepherd Dogs are a hearty, vibrant breed. Part of the health of your dog lies in his breeding—good breeders work hard to make sure their dogs are free of genetic disorders. The rest is up to you. You are responsible for feeding your GSD a proper diet, getting him plenty of exercise, finding a great vet, and keeping up on his annual check-ups.

Finding a Vet

Your German Shepherd Dog will need regular veterinary appointments throughout his life, so having a vet for your dog is just as important as having a doctor for your family. Asking for recommendations from friends is a good place to start your search.

Think about whether you want to take your dog to a multi-vet practice or to a smaller veterinary surgery. The advantage to a smaller practice is that the vet will get to know you and your dog well. The disadvantage is that, in an emergency, if you need to see another vet, he won't know your dog's history or have access to your dog's records. In a multi-vet practice, while you may not see the same vet every visit, all of the vets will have your dog's complete medical history when they need it.

Distance may be a factor as well. You may not mind driving a half hour to see a highly recommended vet, but if there's a life-threatening emergency, you're going to have to also find a practice closer to home.

Call the practices in your area, and ask how they handle emergencies. Is there a vet always on call? Or do several practices work together to provide an out-of-hours service? In the UK emergency veterinary cover must be provided by law.

Visit the veterinary practices. Waiting rooms should be clean, and the staff should be friendly and helpful. Talk to the vet and consider how he or she handles your dog and responds to your questions. Your dog's health care is a partnership between you and the vet. No matter how highly a practice is recommended, if you are uncomfortable for any reason, or your questions and concerns aren't dealt with to your satisfaction, find another vet.

Puppy's First Visit

It's a good idea to have an initial check-up for your GSD puppy. Your puppy will get a physical, much the same as humans get. The vet will listen to his

52

German Shepherd Dogs

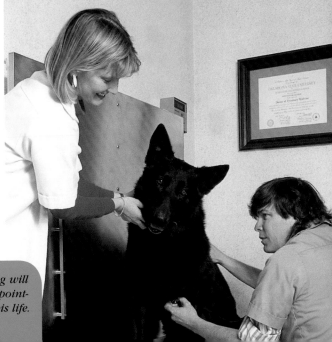

Your German Shepherd Dog will need regular veterinary appointments throughout his life.

heart and lungs, look into his eyes and ears, and check his mouth and throat. If vaccinations are required, your puppy will get the injections during this visit. This is a good time to talk to the vet about any concerns you may have about proper care of your dog. Some vaccines, such as protection against Lyme disease, may be given only if there is a risk in your particular area. If you need help cutting nails or brushing your dog's teeth, this is a good time to get the information you need.

Yearly Check-ups

Yearly check-ups are an important part of keeping your Shepherd healthy. At these check-ups, your dog will get any vaccination booster shots he needs. Yearly visits mean that your vet has a chance to catch problems early. Older dogs may have blood work done each year that may identify a problem before there are any physical signs. No matter what your dog's age, the vet will check his teeth and may recommend a professional cleaning. Just like your puppy's first visit, the vet will check eyes, ears, mouth, heart and lungs.

Vaccinations

Depending on the age of your puppy, he may or may not have received his first set of vaccinations. Currently, many vets give the first set of injections at 8 weeks, followed by a second set a few weeks later, and then annually after that. Before you bring your puppy home, check to see what, if any, vaccinations have been given to him.

The practice of giving every dog

FAMILY-FRIENDLY TIP

Children at the Vet's Office

Consider your child's age before you let him or her accompany you on a visit to the vet. Young children may become upset if they think someone is hurting their dog, and with a German Shepherd Dog, if the child is crying, the dog may think he or she needs protection. Generally speaking, children under seven years old should stay out of the examination room. If an older child is allowed into the consulting room, explain beforehand that your dog's visit to a vet is just like a person visiting a doctor. The vet will look in the dog's ears, eyes and mouth, listen to his heart and lungs, and take the dog's temperature. If your dog will be getting a shot, let your child know that ahead of time. Explain the importance of remaining calm and quiet to help the dog remain calm and quiet.

every kind of vaccination yearly has been challenged in recent years, so you should discuss this issue with your vet. Rather than automatically vaccinating every dog each year, many vets now vaccinate on a case-by-case basis. They

Discuss your GSD's vaccination protocol with your vet.

might vaccinate show dogs or dogs who travel frequently more often than older, stay-at-home dogs.

Currently, drug companies are working on longer-lasting vaccinations—ones that would offer protection for three to four years. Ask your vet, as these vaccinations should soon be available.

Diseases to Vaccinate Against

Most vets give combination vaccinations that include protection against distemper, leptospirosis, hepatitis, parvovirus, and may or may not also include parainfluenza. An innoculation against rabies is required if you are travelling with your dog overseas.

So what exactly are these diseases that your dog may be vaccinated against?

Bordetella

Most boarding kennels require a bordetella, or kennel cough vaccination, and that's a good idea if you're travelling a lot, or showing, as kennel cough is highly contagious. Keep in mind that even with a bordetella shot, your dog may still catch kennel cough. There are over one hundred varieties, and the vaccine only protects against a few of those. Kennel cough can be treated with antibiotics, but is not usually serious.

Coronavirus

Coronavirus is a highly contagious virus that results in diarrhoea for about a week. The diarrhoea may be orange-tinged and will have a strong odour. The disease is rarely fatal, but the dog may need to be treated for dehydration. Talk to your vet about the need for this shot. A healthy, mostly indoor dog might not need this innoculation, but it might be advisable for a show dog, or a dog that regularly comes in contact with many other dogs. Since it is rarely fatal, you might just decide against it.

Distempter

Distemper is a dangerous disease that has a very low recovery rate. The danger from this very contagious virus is greatest in dogs three to six months of age and in dogs over six years of age. Symptoms include vomiting, coughing, fever, and death is the usual outcome.

Hepatitis

Dogs with mild to moderate cases of hepatitis generally have a fever and are lethargic. They may be reluctant to move, have abdominal tenderness, and pale mucous membranes. They will usually recover anywhere from one to five days after showing symptoms. In severe cases, the dog may vomit, have diarrhoea, and develop a cough. Sudden death may result. The disease is spread through the virus in faeces and urine.

Leptospirosis

Leptospirosis is a bacteria frequently transmitted through urine, especially that of rats and mice. Symptoms include vomiting, fever, and a reluctance to move. There may also be signs of renal failure. Severe cases can be fatal. If you live in an area where your dog will be exposed to the urine of rats and mice, you might want to make sure your dog is protected against Leptospirosis. Otherwise, this may be a shot you can skip. Many vets no longer routinely give the Leptospirosis vaccine. Ask your vet about this.

Lyme Disease

The deer tick spreads Lyme disease. Symptoms include lethargy, loss of appetite, and lameness. It is treated with antibiotics. Ask your vet if this disease is a problem in your area. It is rare in the UK but its incidence is increasing.

Vaccination recommendations will depend on where you live or what you're doing with your dog.

Parvovirus

Parvovirus may be fatal, especially if the symptoms include vomiting and bloody diarrhoea. There may be a fever, and the dog will be lethargic and depressed. Dogs with mild cases of the disease generally recover, but young puppies are very susceptible and generally do not survive. This is why those early vaccination injections are so important.

Your puppy should be checked over by a vet as soon as you bring him home.

Between six months and two years, besides finishing off the growth period, your dog will become sexually mature. If you are not seriously committed to showing or breeding, you should neuter your German Shepherd puppy at this time.

Besides the benefit of no unwanted litters, spaying a female before her third heat lowers the chance of mammary tumours. Spaying also ends the chance of pyometra and other reproductive infections as well as the twice yearly "season."

Entire males may be susceptible to prostatic hypertrophy, which is a benign enlargement of the prostate. Castration prevents prostate problems, may curb aggression, and ends marking in the house. As an entire male matures, he will start "lifting his leg" more and more frequently, marking his territory. He may start marking in the house, as well, which can be a very hard habit to break. He may become more aggressive towards other males. He will certainly become more interested in females. If he were to ever get loose, he would be more apt to stray further from home than a neutered male. Castration can help prevent these problems.

Neither spaying nor castration is difficult or particularly hard on a healthy, young dog. Castration is the easier of the two because the testicles are external. If you're worried about appearance, ask the vet about a vasectomy, which is a bit more complicated. Spaying takes a little longer because it is abdominal surgery. After you bring your puppy home, keep an eye on the incision. Redness or puffiness could indicate infection.

There shouldn't be much weight gain in a neutered animal if their exercise level doesn't change. If you notice a weight gain, cut back a bit on your dog's food.

Rabies

Rabies is a virus that attacks the central nervous system of mammals and is spread through saliva. Common carriers in the wild include bats and foxes. Rabies is a fatal disease. Once symptoms appear, there is no cure. Rabies can be prevented by vaccinations, which are required by law in the US. There is no legal requirement in the UK as the disease has been virtually eradicated, except for a few isolated cases.

Potential Reactions

Sometimes, dogs can have negative reactions to vaccines. After your first vaccination, stay at the vet's surgery for a while to see if your German Shepherd Dog is going to have a reaction. If he does, the medical staff will be available to quickly counteract the reaction. If your dog does react to vaccinations, make sure to notify your vet. If he knows this, he might break up the injections for your dog instead of giving a combination. Splitting up the doses doesn't mean your vet is just trying to get more money from you. It means he is concerned about your dog.

Potential Health Issues for the GSD

Almost any dog can be diagnosed with health problems, and the German Shepherd Dog is no exception. While in general this breed is a healthy one, German Shepherd Dogs are prone to bloat/torsion, degenerative myelopathy, and hip dysplasia. They are also more apt to contract Inflammatory Bowel Disease than many other breeds.

Bloat

Many large dogs are at risk for bloat, also called gastric torsion. With bloat, the dog's stomach fills with gas, and the stomach revolves, closing off both the opening from the

Bloat is a problem that affects large dogs.

57

Feeling Good

oesophagus and the opening to the intestines. If your dog is bloating, you may notice his abdomen is distended. He may be pacing, groaning, or otherwise acting uncomfortable. If you think your GSD is bloating, get him to your veterinary surgery immediately. Bloat is fatal if not treated. While no one is exactly sure what causes bloat, it has been suggested to feed two or more smaller meals (instead of one large one) to reduce the risk. And avoid feeding your dog immediately before or after strenuous exercise.

German Shepherd Dogs

Degenerative Myelopathy

Degenerative myelopathy is a disease that affects the hind legs of a dog. The protective sheath (myelin) over the nerves in the lower spinal chord degenerate, and the dog gradually loses the use of his hind legs. At first, you may notice your dog stumbling occasionally. Then his feet may start to drag. He may walk a few steps and fall. Eventually, he will lose the use of his hind legs entirely.

Dogs with degenerative myelopathy are not in pain and are still able to relieve themselves, but as the disease progresses, you may need to support your dog with a sling to help hold up his hindquarters so he can either urinate or defecate. Currently, there is no cure for this disease. Studies have shown that degenerative myelopathy in GSDs may be the result of an altered immune system.

Hip Dysplasia

Hip dysplasia is a condition where the head of the femur does not fit properly into its pelvic socket. There are several degrees of hip dysplasia.

In some dogs, you may never know they are dysplastic, while in others there is severe lameness and pain. Surgery can correct the problem, but it's very expensive. To manage the lameness and pain, talk to your vet about some of the medicines that are now available. If the degree of dysplasia is slight, even an aspirin can help make your dog more comfortable.

Conscientious breeders will have their breeding stock X-rayed and evaluated for this condition, but there is no guarantee that your dog might not still suffer from hip dysplasia. Rapid growth in puppies may contribute to hip dysplasia, which is one reason many breeders recommend feeding an adult food right away rather than higher-protein puppy food.

Many dogs with hip dsyplasia can still be active family members. You may not be able to compete in agility or advanced sports with a dysplastic dog, but you can still do basic obedience, as well as just playing with your dog in the garden. An aspirin after a busy day may be all that's needed if your dog is a bit lame.

Inflammatory Bowel Disease (IBD)

Inflammatory bowel disease is sometimes confused with Irritable Bowel Syndrome (IBS), but IBS is a stress-related problem. IBD results when the wall of the large intestine is invaded by the dog's own inflammatory cells. This invasion causes a thickening of the lining, which interferes with the ability of the bowel to both absorb and to contract. The most common symptoms are diarrhoea and vomiting. Other symptoms may include weight loss, depression, abdominal pain, and fever. IBD may be the result of parasites, allergies, genetics, or nutrition, so treating it becomes a process of elimination. A vet may put a dog on a hypo-allergenic diet for a few months, and he may also suggest a diet with fewer fats and more fibre. IBD may also be treated with medication and/or vitamin B supplements.

Other Common Issues

Any dog of any breed can suffer from pests or cancer. Regular check-ups can help prevent many conditions and can

Pet Insurance

Insurance for pets is now available. Basic coverage typically includes accidents and major illnesses. It does not usually cover general office visits, vaccinations, or spaying or castration. Basic insurance may also have a cap on it for illnesses such as cancer; and many insurance policies won't cover advanced medical techniques or, if they do, they require a special rider to the base policy. Most insurance policies won't cover pre-existing conditions, so if your dog is diagnosed with cancer, for instance, you won't be able to insure your dog.

catch problems early, while they're still small.

Fleas and Ticks

Fleas and ticks are nasty little parasites that, besides sucking your dog's blood, can transmit diseases. Fleas may transmit worms, and ticks can cause Lyme disease in rare cases.

Many dogs are allergic to flea saliva, which can cause them to scratch incessantly. To check for fleas, roll your dog over and inspect his stomach where the fur is thinner, especially back toward the hind legs. If you see fleas fleeing, the war has begun. If you don't see a flea, you may find "flea dirt"—dark flecks that will turn red when placed on a dampened paper towel. If you don't find any fleas or dirt, but still suspect fleas, comb your dog with a flea comb. The fine teeth of the comb can trap fleas lurking in your dog's coat.

If your dog has hundreds of fleas, a bath with flea shampoo will help initially and then you should consider a monthly preventative. Talk to your vet about what is best for your dog. If you live in an area where ticks are also a problem, there are products that deal with both types of parasite.

Wash your dog's bed regularly. That's where the flea eggs will be. Cut up a flea collar and put it in your

The Expert Knows

How to Remove a Tick

Ticks are nasty little parasites that can spread disease to both you and your pet. If you find a tick on your dog, use tweezers to remove the tick. Grasp firmly near where the tick is attached to your dog and pull gently and slowly. Don't crush, jerk, or squeeze the tick. Applying alcohol may make the tick back out on its own. Don't handle the tick. If you do touch the tick, wash your hands immediately. Once you've removed the tick, wash the area where it was embedded in your dog, and then disinfect. Be sure you have removed the whole tick and not left the mouthparts embedded in your dog's skin, as this can cause infection.

vacuum cleaner to help kill whatever fleas you vacuum up. Also remember to change your vacuum bag and empty your vacuum cleaner frequently, or you could end up with a colony of fleas living and breeding inside your cleaner.

Ticks can be harder to detect. Make a habit of running your hands over your dog once or twice a week. You may feel a bump that is a well-fed tick. Push your dog's fur back against the grain, and check the skin for ticks. If ticks are a problem in your area, consider a preventative, and ask your vet if your dog needs the Lyme disease vaccine.

Cancer

The bad news is that cancer can strike any dog. The good news is that 50 percent of all cancers can be cured, and progress is being made in treating the other 50 percent. Your dog may get a tumour, or cancer may strike the bone or the lymph nodes. If you discover an odd growth that is growing rapidly, don't wait. Get your dog to the vet. If you notice swollen lymph nodes, don't wait. If your dog is limping, seems tired all the time, or is vomiting for more than 24 hours, don't wait.

Surgery may rid the body of a cancer, or chemotherapy may, if not cure it, at least put it in remission, buying your dog some more time. Radiation therapy is also a possibility.

First Aid

German Shepherd Dogs are generally healthy, but there are things to watch for in any dog.

When to Call the Vet

Any problem that persists longer than 24 hours is reason to call your

Learning first aid can help save your dog's life.

Feeling Good

vet. Also, any problem that worsens over several hours or produces loss of appetite, weakness, or fever needs prompt medical attention. If your dog has a mild case of diarrhoea or vomits once or twice, stop all food for a day and give only water. You may want to feed cooked ground meat with rice for a day or two. If there are frequent bouts of vomiting or diarrhoea, or if it continues for more than 24 hours, call the vet.

A dog's normal temperature is between 100 and 102°F. If the temperature goes above 104°F, or below 100°F, call the vet. If the dog is bleeding and the blood is spurting, or can't be stopped by pressure, call the vet.

If you suspect poisoning, don't wait! Call the vet immediately. Your vet may give you advice over the telephone or may ask you to bring the dog to the surgery straight away. It will be a big advantage if you know what your dog ate. Take along any relevant packaging to the surgery. If you need to induce vomiting, you can do so by administering hydrogen peroxide, but do not do this unless advised, and certainly not if the substance is unknown. Caustic products, such as many household cleaners, will cause more damage when the dog vomits. Give the dog lots of milk or vegetable oil.

Choking

You may never need to administer first aid to your dog, but there are some things that you should know

German Shepherd Dogs

SENIOR DOG TIP

Health of Your Older GSD

Generally speaking, a dog becomes a veteran around the age of seven, even though you may not notice any outwards signs. Your dog may still play just as hard and eat just as well, but that doesn't mean that your dog isn't ageing. When he turns seven or eight, it's time to include a blood screen test with those annual visits to the vet. This testing will tell your vet what's going on with your dog's pancreas, liver, and kidneys. It may alert him to a problem before there are any outward symptoms, and the earlier a problem is detected, the more likely there'll be a cure, or at least a slowing down of a problem.

Pay attention to your older dog's eating and toileting habits. If there's a drastic change, notify your vet. Your dog may start to show signs of arthritis, so tell your vet if your dog is occasionally lame or seems unusually stiff when he gets up from a nap. A veteran dog may still be just as active as he ever was and paying more attention to his health will help keep him that way.

just in case. Find out about animal first aid courses, which can help you understand just what you can do to help your pet until you can reach the vet.

If your dog is choking on something, use the handle of a screwdriver between the back teeth to keep mouth open and prevent the dog from biting as you check out his throat and mouth. If you can see the object causing the problem, use your fingers, or a pair of needle-nosed pliers to remove it. If you can't reach it, hold your dog upside down by the hind legs and shake him. If that doesn't work, apply forceful, sudden pressure to the abdomen at the edge of the breastbone. (Use your fist—think Heimlich manoeuvre.)

Other Injuries

In case of a major emergency, such as a dogfight or your dog being hit by a car, it is natural to panic, but you need

Keep an eye on your dog when he's outside in extreme cold or heat.

injury to the dog and possibly injury to you.

Muzzle

When a dog is hurt, frightened, in pain, he is apt to snap blindly at any touch, even yours. A muzzle will protect you and make it easier to treat and transport your dog. You can buy a nylon muzzle from a pet supply store or catalogue, or you can use a length of gauze from the roll in the first aid kit.

To properly apply a muzzle of gauze (or rope or a lead if necessary), make a loop by tying a half-knot in the gauze. Place the loop over the dog's muzzle with the half-knot on top. It will probably be easier to do if you are behind the dog and will also lessen the chance of a bite. Tighten the knot, and bring the ends of gauze under the muzzle. Make another half knot, then bring the ends up behind the dog's ears and tie a bow or other quick release knot. Now you can examine or transport your German Shepherd Dog without fear of being bitten.

If your dog is having trouble breathing, don't use a muzzle, which may restrict his efforts to breathe. Instead, try to restrain your dog with a blanket or some other kind of padding

to stay calm for the sake of your dog. In spite of the voice in your head telling you to hurry, slow down and take a moment to think about what your best course of action should be. All too often, improper handling on the spur of the moment can result in further that extends around his head and beyond his nose several inches. This will not totally eliminate the chance of a bite, but it will help.

Transporting an Injured Animal

The best way to transport an injured animal is on a blanket or a board, especially if any spinal cord injury is suspected. Get help, if possible, and try to shift the dog all at once to the blanket or board. Try to move him as little as possible. Call your vet and give him a brief description of your dog's injuries and tell him you are on the way. Although you may feel calling the veterinary surgery is wasting time, your call gives them the time they need to prepare for the emergency. Take the time to call ahead.

With time and practice, you will not panic over minor problems but will learn when you can wait and when you need to make an emergency visit to the veterinary surgery. When in doubt, always call your vet. He can offer the help and reassurance you need.

Holistic Therapies

Today, some veterinary practices are going beyond the bounds of traditional medicine to offer you and your pet as many treatment options as possible. Holistic vets are becoming more and more popular. Webster defines holistic as "emphasising the organic" so you would expect a holistic vet to use natural substances in healing, and they do. But many holistic vets use a combination of techniques and medicines in an attempt to treat the whole dog and not just symptoms. A combination of Western medicine, homeopathy, and traditional Chinese medicine may be recommended. In some cases, a vet may refer you to a specialist in a particular therapy who will be able to treat your dog most effectively.

Acupuncture

Acupuncture has been practiced on humans in China for more than 4,500 years and on animals for about 2,000 years. Using hair-fine needles, an acupuncturist stimulates appropriate acupoints to help with healing. Acupoints are tiny areas on the skin that contain relatively concentrated levels of nerve endings, lymphatics, and blood vessels.

Studies have shown that acupuncture can increase blood flow, lower heart rate, and improve immune function. Acupuncture also stimulates the release of certain neurotransmitters like endorphins, the body's natural painkillers, and smaller amounts of cortisal, an anti-

65

Don't use any natural remedy on your dog until you've spoken to your vet.

inflammatory steroid.

Acupuncture is commonly used for treating chronic conditions like arthritis and allergies, and to relieve pain and inflammation. Epilepsy may also be helped by acupuncture.

If you want to learn more about acupuncture or want to find a vet in your area who practices acupuncture, you can read books on the subject or get information on the Internet.

Chiropractic

Chiropractic treatment may also help your dog, especially if you and he are very active. Bones may get out of position in relation to one another or may not be moving properly because of a fall or bumping into something. Chiropractic treatment re-aligns those bones. Most commonly, the spine may need alignment, especially if your dog leaps and twists in play. An adjustment may be just what your Shepherd needs to keep zipping around that agility course. Find a vet who not only offers chiropractic services but will also know if some other form of treatment is needed.

Flower Essences

Flower essences, also known as Bach flower essences, are meant to treat emotional problems, such as fear of noise or shyness. Rescue Remedy, which is a mixture of five remedies, is effective in cases of shock, collapse, and trauma. Many holistic vets will suggest Rescue Remedy as a part of your dog's first aid kit. Check your local health food store for this product.

Herbs

Some holistic vets use herbs in their practice. Herbal medicines overall may be gentler and safer (when properly administered) than extracts or synthetic compounds. This does not mean you should dash off to the chemist and give your GSD herbal tablets. Consult with a vet who understands the correct way to use herbs to help with the healing process.

Homeopathy

Homeopathy is based on the theory that "like heals like." A substance is diluted in several stages so that is it safe and free from side effects, yet is still powerful enough to act as a healing agent. According to *New Choices in Natural Healing for Dogs and Cats,* there are more than 3,000 homeopathic remedies in use. These come in tablets, powders, granules, liquids, and ointments.

While you may not feel comfortable with every type of alternative to traditional veterinary care, you may come to appreciate a vet who is willing to look at all forms of treatment to give the best health care to his patients. Many alternatives are, in fact, complementary to traditional medicine.

SENIOR DOG TIP

Coping With a Veteran's Declining Health

Coping with an older dog's declining health may be as simple as giving him a child's aspirin at the end of the day or making sure he sleeps on an elevated bed in a draught-free area. It may mean you need to build a ramp from your porch to the ground because he can no longer navigate stairs. He may start to lose his eyesight or his hearing, and you'll need to help him compensate for those losses. Your vet may prescribe a specific medicine or a special food. Your dog may need to go out to relieve himself more frequently, and he may be slower to obey commands. A senior dog means a bit more work, but it's worth it. Your dog has given you years of love and devotion; now it's time for you to pay back some of that devotion and make him as comfortable as you can.

Feeling Good

Chapter 6

Being Good

German Shepherd Dogs are big dogs and need training. An untrained dog is no fun to live with, and no one's going to be happy about visiting your home if there's an untrained GSD bouncing all over, jumping up, barking, and stealing food. Training starts with you becoming a good leader to your dog. All dogs are pack animals, and to a dog, the family is his pack. If there is no leader, your dog will try to fill the position, so you need to let him know that you set the rules, not him.

Make sure that everyone in the family is consistent about what the dog is allowed to do. It's confusing to the dog and counter-productive if Mum and the kids don't allow the dog to jump on them, but Dad encourages it. Consistency and good leadership will help create a well-behaved family pet.

Socialisation means getting your GSD used to different types of animals, people, and situations.

Socialisation

Before starting any kind of formal training, your dog should be socialised. German Shepherd Dogs are by nature protective and may be aloof, but they should never be shy or fearful. Socialisation means introducing your puppy to as many new and different situations as possible. Put your dog's crate in a part of the house that sees a lot of activity like the kitchen or the family room. Let him get used to the sounds of dinner being prepared, the phone ringing, the kettle whistling. Let him hear the television or a radio. Have family and friends pet and play with him. Introduce him to different toys and to different surfaces underfoot. All these things help to build confidence in your puppy.

Once your GSD has his initial vaccinations, take him for walks around the neighbourhood. Encourage people to gently pet your puppy. If you don't have children, find some who are willing to gently play with him. Children, with their sudden movements and high-pitched voices, may frighten a dog, and a frightened GSD can be dangerous. Take your dog with you when you run errands. Sit on a bench at a shopping mall; carry extra treats, and ask some of the people passing to give the treats to your dog.

Expose your dog to different types of people. Take your German Shepherd Dog to a playground, and let him see bicycles and skateboards. If there's a dog park in your neighbourhood—even if you don't feel you can let your dog loose—visit the park and get your GSD used to seeing other dogs. If you have a friend or neighbour with a sociable dog, introduce the dogs. Make the introductions on neutral ground, keep the dogs leaded, and make the introduction slowly.

If there are no dog parks and no neighbourhood dogs that are good candidates as playmates, enroll in a puppy socialisation class or an obedience class so that your German Shepherd Dog can get used to being around other dogs.

Housetraining

German Shepherd Dogs housetrain easily, but they can't do it alone. It's up to you to have a schedule and to be consistent. One of the best ways to housetrain is to use a crate. Dogs don't like to soil their own beds, and given a chance, a puppy will learn to hold it until he is taken outside. The other advantage to a crate is that it is a

FAMILY-FRIENDLY TIP

Children and Training

Children should be a part of your German Shepherd Dog's training. Older children will benefit from attending classes. If only one person can attend a class, that person should teach the others in the family, and everyone should work with the dog. Just make sure training is consistent, and everyone is doing the same thing. Even very small children should be able to ask a dog to sit with the aid of a treat. Just remember to always supervise small children and dogs.

Being Good

Finding a Trainer

Class situations are a good way to both socialise your dog and get him used to distractions. There are training clubs in most areas of the country.

If possible, see if you can attend a class as an observer. Stay away from anyone who advocates hitting the dog or lifting him off his feet by the lead. You want to look for a trainer who uses positive reinforcement to teach your dog.

Observe the size of the class. The larger the class, the less individual attention you'll receive.

Talk to friends and neighbours who may have taken obedience classes, or see if your vet knows of a local class.

If you want private lessons, get referrals. Talk to people who've hired a particular instructor.

small, easy-to-clean surface, so if your puppy does have an accident, it's easier to clean than the rug and causes less damage.

Whenever you take your puppy out to relieve himself, take him on lead. With a lead, you can direct him to the spot in the garden where you'd like him to go, and you can help him focus on why you're out there. Puppies can get easily distracted and forget to do their business.

When you take your puppy out, choose a word or phrase that will be your puppy's cue to 'go.' It could be "hurry up," or "be busy" or anything at all. Once your dog is housetrained, this phrase can come in handy. If you're going somewhere for a few hours, take your dog out, say the command phrase and your dog should relieve himself. Then you can leave him alone at home without worrying about accidents.

Schedule

Take your puppy out first thing in the morning. Carry him outside—don't coax him to follow you through the house because he probably won't make it; and the fewer mistakes made indoors, the faster the housetraining will be.

Once your puppy has gone, take him back inside for breakfast. Crate him, or put him in his area while you eat, then take him back outside 20 to 30 minutes after he's eaten. Give him some playtime, and then take him out one more time. Crate him for no more than four hours.

Don't punish your puppy for housetraining mistakes.

He'll need to be taken out around lunchtime. If no one can get home for lunch, see if there's a neighbour who can help. Take the puppy out, then give him his lunch, some playtime, another trip out, and then back in the crate. If you have children, they should take the puppy out when they get home from school. No matter who takes the puppy out, make sure everyone knows how important it is to get the puppy out quickly so he has a chance to relieve himself in the proper area. Puppies may sniff and circle, but sometimes they just squat and go, so make sure you pay attention.

After dinner, your puppy should go out again and then have another play session. Each puppy is different, but puppies, like babies, need lots of sleep, so your German Shepherd Dog may sleep all evening while you're watching television. Take him out one last time at about 11 p.m. If he's kept warm all night, he should be fine until you are up at 6 a.m. to start the day. If your puppy gets cold during the night, he'll wake up, and if he wakes up, he'll have to go. Crate your puppy in someone's bedroom so if he does wake up, someone will hear him and can take him out.

House training may take until the puppy is 12 to 16 weeks old or possibly longer, depending on the puppy, but it's not something that can be rushed. Also,

Consistently bring your puppy to the designated outdoor toilet spot.

even if your puppy seems reliable at 16 weeks, there may be lapses. If someone is home with the puppy, he can probably have the run of the house, but if you're going out don't leave the puppy loose. Take the precaution of putting him in his crate or in a safe room.

Paper Training

If no one can get home in the middle of the day, you'll need to paper train your puppy. Choose a room for confining the puppy. It could be your kitchen, bathroom, or laundry room. If the room is too large to easily cover the floor with newspapers, you can block off a section. Put the puppy's crate, toys, and water bowl in the chosen area. When you are home, try to follow the schedule as discussed under using the crate. Take the puppy out after naps, after meals, and after playtime. When unattended, place the puppy in the papered area. When you clean up, remove the top layers of paper and replace with fresh. After a week or so, reduce the area covered by paper. If the puppy successfully uses the paper and not the uncovered floor, reduce the area even further. Continue until all the papers have been picked up.

Accidents Happen

When cleaning up after your puppy, never use any cleaning product that contains ammonia. Puppies tend to return to whatever spot they've used before, and scent tells them they've come to the right place. Urine contains ammonia so if you wash with an ammonia-based cleaner, that residue will tell the puppy he's in the right place. Club soda works well to help prevent staining, and white vinegar helps deodorise. The oxygen-based cleaners that are now on the market are also very good.

Never punish your puppy for mistakes. If you catch him in the act, scoop him up and rush him outside. Praise him when he goes in the right place. Yelling at him after the fact does no good at all. Housetraining takes patience, observation, and consistency on your part.

Basic Commands

Besides having a well-socialised, housetrained dog, your GSD should

Treats for Training

When using treats for training, remember that those treats are part of your dog's daily allowance of food. Cut the treats up into tiny pieces so you can reward often and not overfeed your dog. Use something soft that your dog can chew and swallow quickly, not something hard and crunchy. Leftover bits of chicken or beef, or morsels of cheese are good choices. Cooked liver can also be cut up small and offered. There are also many commercial dog treats on the market that are soft, but you'll want to cut up even the "bite sized" treats. The food is a lure and a reward, not a meal, and shouldn't be in large chunks.

calm. If your dog is licking his nose, yawning, or shaking himself, he is using signals to break the tension. Look around to see what might have him worried.

- Aggression. If a dog is aggressive, everything about him leans forward and gets bigger. Ears will be up and forward, the dog will be on his toes. His hackles will rise. His tail will be up and will be stiff. If the dog is snarling, his nose will be wrinkled. He will be staring.

- Playfulness. Dogs use a play bow to indicate that they are in the mood for a game. In a play bow, the front half of the body is lowered so that the forelegs are on the ground, leaving the rear end in the air. The tail will be wagging, and the dog may give a high-pitched bark or two. They may pant.

Dogs are masters at interpreting body language, and they "read" other dogs as well as humans. You should learn to understand some of your German Shepherd Dog's body language. It will help you understand him better and make training easier.

- Fear. A dog with his tail tucked between his legs may be frightened. He is definitely submissive. He is telling other dogs, and you, that he is no threat to anyone. He will also avert his eyes, plaster his ears back, and hold his head low.

- Anxiety/stress. A dog may also be anxious or stressed in this position, and he may be panting. Dogs who are worried may sit with one paw raised. A yawn briefly lowers a dog's blood pressure and helps him stay

As much as dogs depend on body language to communicate with other dogs, they are also close observers of human body language. Standing tall and looming over a dog is a sign of dominance. When you stand tall, lean over your dog, or even put your arm across his back, you are saying you are dominant. Conversely, if a strange dog is nervous and shy, you can help by crouching down, turning sideways to appear smaller, and not making eye contact. Staring is a form of both dominance and aggression.

know some basic commands. You can start training these to your German Shepherd Dog right away.

Training used to mean using a training collar with a lead and frequently pushing or pulling your dog into the position you desired. Today, most training methods focus on positive training using food rewards. Keep the treats small; you're just tempting your dog, not feeding him dinner.

Keep your training sessions short and happy. Three or four short sessions of five minutes is more effective than one session of 20 minutes, especially with a puppy.

Always end a training session on a positive note. If you're trying to teach your dog a specific behaviour, and he just isn't getting it, don't continue. Both you and your dog will get frustrated. Instead, ask your dog to do something it already knows how to do: sit, down, or come. Ask your dog to do it, and then give him a treat, praise him, and end the lesson.

Come

Your dog needs to come when called. If he accidentally gets out or is in a dangerous situation, he needs to respond to the come command. Have some treats

ready, and call your puppy. Sound happy and excited. If his attention wanders, run away from your puppy, calling his name. When he comes, give him a treat and praise him.

Never call your dog for punishment or for something he may find unpleasant. Call him to dinner, not to clip his nails. No matter how frustrated your GSD may make you when you're in a hurry and he won't come in, when you do get him be gentle and praise him. He must associate good things with obeying the come command.

Sit

Sitting is probably the easiest thing you can teach a dog. Hold a treat in front of your GSD's nose, and slowly move

When teaching the come command, keep your dog on a long lead and call to him.

it back over the top of his head. Don't hold it too high or he'll be tempted to jump up. As the treat moves back, give the sit command. The dog will sit as he tries to follow the treat with his eyes and nose. The instant he sits, give him the treat and tell him how wonderful he is.

The sit command can be useful in many situations. Tell your dog to sit before you put his food dish down so he isn't crowding in and spilling food. A sit when your Shepherd comes in from the yard gives you a chance to wipe off muddy paws. Have your dog sit before a guest pets him—German Shepherds are big dogs and may intimidate some people. A sitting dog is less threatening, and the petting becomes a reward for

the sit. When it's time for a walk, it's easier to snap a lead on your dog's collar when he's sitting quietly than when he's dancing for joy at the prospect of a walk.

Stay

Next, you might want to teach your German Shepherd Dog to stay. Start with your dog sitting on your left. Place your open palm in front of his nose and say, "Stay." Advance one step directly in front of the dog, then move back beside him, praise, and treat. Gradually extend the amount of time you are in front of him before you release him. As he seems to understand the command, move backward a step or two. If he breaks from the sit, gently replace him, repeat the stay command, and step away. Don't try to go too fast, don't lose your temper, and keep the lesson short and happy.

Remember that even games can be a way to teach your dog. Try putting your dog on a stay, going to another room, and calling him. Don't expect too much at first, but eventually your GSD will be doing a sit-stay while you're out of sight.

A dog who obeys the stay

Your dog can learn the sit command quite easily.

command gets to remain with the family rather than be shut in another room or crated. Put your dog on a down-stay when you're munching a snack, and you won't have to constantly defend your food from a begging dog. Put your dog on a sit or a down stay during dinner, and no one

SENIOR DOG TIP

Training the Older Dog

It's not true that you can't teach an old dog new tricks. You can. What is true is that an older dog may not be able to move as quickly as a younger dog. Stiff hindquarters may mean a slower sit, or the dog may sit crookedly to accommodate sore joints. When you call an older dog, he may walk or trot rather than gallop. Use the same training techniques with your senior, but give him a bit more time to respond. An older dog may not hear as well as a young dog, so you may want to use hand signals to train a dog who is going deaf.

will be tempted to slip him a bit of chicken. Tell your dog to stay, and you can open the front door and retrieve the mail without your dog escaping.

The stay command can come in handy when you're trying to keep your dog out of dangerous situations. One day I was taking something out of the oven, and my dog approached the open, hot door. I used the stay command to keep him from away until it was safe. The stay command is also good if you break a glass—give the command in your best "leader of the pack" voice and your GSD will not come into the room and get paws full of glass.

Down

Down is a little harder to teach. Many books and many instructors will tell you that once your dog is sitting, you just take a treat and slowly move it down toward his feet and out a bit. The dog will slide into the down. I've seen this work with many breeds, but I've also noticed that some dogs just pop right up onto all four feet.

One of the best ways to teach down to a German Shepherd Dog is to teach him a few other commands first, so he understands the concept of learning something. Then, try a down. Tell your Shepherd to sit. Hold a treat in your hand and move it slowly down and away as you give the command to down. If he slides into the down, terrific. Give him lots of praise and the treat. Instead of sliding into the down, he may jump up and go after the hand holding the treat. Don't let him get the treat. He may paw at your hand, or even nibble at it, trying to get the treat. He may sit again. Be patient. Eventually he will lie down, and that's when you quickly give him the treat and praise him.

Down works much like sit, except that if you want your dog to remain in one place for a longer period of time, the down is more comfortable and relaxing. A down-stay works better during a dinner party, for instance; whereas, if you just want your dog to hold still while you snap on his lead, a sit works well, and you don't have to bend over.

Walking on a Lead

You should get your puppy used to a collar and lead even if you have a fenced garden. There will be times and places when you'll want to be able to walk your dog, and there will certainly be trips to the vet.

First, get your puppy used to the lead. Fasten a light lead to his collar and let him drag it along. Do this only when you're supervising. You don't want the lead to snag on

Teach your GSD to walk on a lead without pulling.

German Shepherd Dogs are intelligent and can learn tricks easily.

something. Pick up the end of the lead, and encourage your puppy to follow you by using a happy voice and treats. If your puppy stops or veers off in another direction, encourage him to return to you. Do not tug, pull, or yank at him. When your GSD understands that the lead is connecting the two of you, try short walks. If he pulls, stop walking. He'll likely turn around and look at you, wondering why you're not following. When the lead is slack, start walking again. If he pulls again, repeat the process.

You can use treats to convince your German Shepherd that walking next to you—or at least close enough to keep the lead slack—is a good idea. I keep my dog interested by randomly saying her name and throwing her a treat. Besides keeping her close, this is a good way to get her attention if there are distractions.

Tricks

It's always fun to have a dog who knows a trick or two, and German Shepherd Dogs will learn quickly. Find a good book on trick training, and you'll soon have your very own circus dog. Remember, there's almost always more than one way to train your dog, so find the way that works best for both of you.

Start with teaching your dog to shake hands. One way to do that is to face your dog with a treat in your hand. Move your hand to the dog's left. As he turns his head to follow your hand, he will also lean left, lifting his right paw a bit. Click and treat if you are using a clicker—if not, just treat. Gradually withhold the click and treat until he is lifting his paw higher.

Many tricks are based on what a dog is naturally inclined to do. My female seemed to go into the "beg" or "sit pretty" position naturally, so she learned quickly to do it on command. Smaller dogs have better balance for "sitting pretty," but your Shepherd can do it too, as long as you don't expect him to hold it for too long. To get your dog to "beg" or "sit pretty,"

have him sit, then, slowly move a hand holding a treat back over his head and up. Don't hold your hand too far up, or he may just leap for the treat. Give your command, and as your dog's front feet leave the ground, treat, or click and treat, if you are using a clicker. Eventually, your dog will be sitting up on his haunches with his front feet off the ground.

If your dog enjoys running and jumping, teach him to jump through a hoop. Place the edge of the hoop on the ground and encourage your dog to walk through, using treats. When your dog is comfortable with the hoop, raise it an inch or so. Go slowly, and don't rush this. Praise and treat. Every other day or so, raise the hoop another couple of inches. Give the command to jump, and praise your dog when he does or click and treat.

Clicker Training

Clicker training is a good way to train your dog using only positive methods. The clickers used for training are available at most pet supply stores. To use this method, whenever your dog does something you want him to do, click and treat. The clicker marks the behaviour at the instant it occurs. There's no delay as there might be with a word of praise and a treat, so your GSD knows exactly what behaviour you are rewarding. Also, the clicker sound is the same every time. There's no edge of impatience, no variation in volume or tone of your voice.

The thing to remember about clicker training is that you must click as you get the behaviour. If you've got an instructor in your area who uses clicker training, talk to him or her about how best to use it. To understand the principles behind clicker training, read Karen Pryor's book, *Don't Shoot the Dog: The New Art of Teaching and Training*. *Clicker Training For Dogs*, also by Karen Pryor, is another good book for beginners.

Chapter 7

In the
Doghouse

Many of the problems people have with their dogs is just normal dog behaviour that, for one reason or another, may not be acceptable to a family or to other people. Barking is normal dog behaviour, but very few people want to listen to a dog bark hour after hour. Dogs dig, but a hole in the middle of a garden or a previously perfect flowerbed becomes a problem. A dog may jump up to greet friends, but if his paws are muddy, it's a problem. Chewing is also normal dog behaviour, but if the chew toy of choice is a pair of good shoes or the leg of an antique chair, the behaviour becomes a problem.

First, depending on the problem, a visit to the vet may be in order to rule out any medical problem. Second, while you may issue a sharp "no" to discourage specific behaviour, never hit your dog. Hitting will not solve the problem and may aggravate it. If you are present when unacceptable behaviour occurs, you may be able to redirect your dog's attention. For instance, if his jaws are clamping down on the leg of that antique chair, trade him the chair for a chew toy.

Third, many behaviours that are considered unacceptable are the result of boredom or too much excess energy. A tired dog is a well-behaved dog. If your dog is going to be alone for an extended period, try to give him a brisk walk with a little jogging thrown in, or if there's time tire him out playing fetch. That may be all it takes to solve the problem.

Make sure your dog is getting enough exercise— pent up energy can cause unwanted behaviours.

Barking (Excessive)

Any dog may bark out of boredom if he is left alone too long. Your German Shepherd Dog shouldn't be left outdoors unattended for long periods of time, but if he barks every time he is in the garden even if for only a few minutes, it can become annoying. Think about installing a solid fence. Dogs rarely bark at things they can't see. If that's not possible, consider planting shrubs to screen the road or neighbour's garden. Give your dog interesting toys or play with him yourself when he's in the garden.

Indoors, if your Shepherd is barking more than you'd like, there are a couple of ways you can curb the barking. One way is to teach your dog to bark on command. Once he knows how to bark on command, you can also teach a command to stop the barking. When your dog barks, click and treat. Name the action (for example, "Speak"). Then choose a word or phrase that tells him to be quiet (for example, "No bark"). When he does stop, click and treat.

If your dog barks every time someone comes to the door, get a friend to help you. Have this person knock on the door. Give the command, "No bark," and when your GSD stops barking, open the door. Have your friend treat the dog. Repeat the process. While you may appreciate the fact that your dog lets you know someone is at the door, he should stop when you tell him to.

If the problem is that your dog barks when no one is home, it may be because he is anxious. This problem is difficult and can take a long time to correct. Start by leaving the house. Close the door, then re-

enter immediately. Praise the dog and treat. Leave again, count to five, then go back in. This is a slow process, but eventually, your dog will realise that you are not leaving for good. You can also try leaving your GSD with a toy that dispenses treats when he plays with it, or get one you can stuff with cheese or peanut butter. This type of toy gives your dog something to do, besides realising that you're gone and he's alone.

Chewing

All puppies chew, especially when they are teething. They may find a chair rung or a table leg suits them just fine, but that probably won't be your first

The Expert Knows

Aggression and Separation Anxiety

You may be able to deal with separation anxiety yourself by supplying lots of toys to keep the dog's mind off being alone, but some separation anxiety leads to destructive behaviour, and you may not be able to deal with this alone. It's time to talk to a professional.

If your dog is aggressive, ask your vet to give your dog a thorough check-up to eliminate any physical problems that might cause aggression. If your dog is fine physically, contact a professional to help you deal with the aggression, and do it immediately.

Give your puppy plenty of appropriate items to chew on.

choice. Offer appropriate items for him to chew on, like rubber chews or nylon bones. If, in spite of all the best toys, your puppy insists on chewing furniture, crate him when you won't be home to watch him.

Older dogs enjoy chewing as well but are usually more willing to chew on a hard rubber toy or a nylon bone.

Be careful with rawhide bones, because while some dogs have no problem with them, other dogs will chew off big chunks and swallow them, which can lead to intestinal problems. If you want to give your dog the occasional real bone, make sure it is fresh and uncooked, and supervise the chewing session. After a day or two, discard the bone. The older the bone, the more it dries out, becoming more apt to

splinter and pose a danger to your dog should he swallow the pieces.

Digging

Almost all puppies will dig a bit, but it's something they usually outgrow. If your German Shepherd Dog continues to enjoy digging holes, designate a special area of the garden for digging. You might even want to create his own little sandbox. If he digs outside of his special spot, distract him with a toy and lead him to the correct spot. Lightly bury a few smelly treats in the permitted spot and when he digs them up, praise him. Sometimes dogs dig because they are bored. Play with your dog in the garden, or supply a toy or a bone that he enjoys.

Housetraining accidents

A young dog who relieves himself in the house may never have been properly housetrained. If that's the case, treat him just as you would a puppy. Use a crate, or close off a room or a section of a room, and follow the housetraining steps in Chapter 6. If an older dog who has previously been reliable in the house starts to have accidents, make an appointment with your vet to make sure there is no physical problem.

If your dog gets a clean bill of health, consider your schedule. Has something changed so that your dog is not being let out at regular intervals? What is the age of your dog? If he's old, he may need more frequent breaks.

If you've just adopted an older dog, the lapse may be temporary because of the stress of a new home and a new family. If the problem continues, make that appointment with the vet, and if the dog has no health problems, begin

FAMILY-FRIENDLY TIP

Safety First

If your dog has a problem behaviour you need to be extra careful concerning children. Depending on what the problem behaviour of the dog is, there may be no safe way for a child to interact independently with the dog. With a small child, whose face is level with a dog's mouth, don't take a chance that everything will be fine. Never leave a small child alone with a dog.

housetraining just as you would with a puppy.

Jumping Up

Jumping can be a bad habit, and unfortunately it is one that is easily learned. People with small dogs usually don't mind if their dog jumps on them, but GSDs are definitely not small, and can knock over a child or an elderly adult. Even if you don't mind your German Shepherd Dog jumping up when you're playing with him, you might not be as happy about the jumping if you're wearing good clothes and your dog has muddy feet. Besides, let's face it, not all your friends will think your dog is as wonderful as you do. Teach your dog to jump up on you on command, if you want to. Otherwise, discourage this behaviour. If you have a friend or relative who is a frequent visitor, get them to help.

If your GSD jumps up, have your friend turn sideways and ignore the dog. Tell your dog to sit. When he does, have your friend pet him. Only give him attention when he sits, not when he is jumping. If you pay attention to your dog when he jumps up on you, you are reinforcing the jumping.

An animal behaviourist may be able to help you with a problem you can't handle on your own.

Nipping

German Shepherd Dogs are a herding breed, which means they instinctively nip at the heels of other animals to get them to move. This nipping may carry over to human ankles. Realise that this is not aggressive behaviour, and also realise that it may be a hard habit to break. Try to determine if the nipping is indeed instinctive or if your dog is nipping because he is irritated or angry. A dog who has never nipped before, but is now nipping, may have a physical problem. A dog with sore joints may nip when he is touched because it hurts. A thorough check up may help you determine if there is a physical cause. If it's not physical, you may need to consult with an animal behaviourist.

Finding a Behaviourist

An animal behaviourist is not the same as a dog trainer. There are many good trainers who are not behaviour specialists. Depending on the severity of the problem, a good trainer may be able to help you, even if he or she isn't a behaviour specialist. If you find you really need a behaviour specialist, start your search by talking to your vet, who should be able to refer you to a specialist. You can also try talking to people at your local training club who may have had experience working with behaviourists. Unfortunately, there is no national standard for certification at this point, so you'll need to consider credentials and get references. Ask to talk to former clients of the specialist.

If you can't find a behaviourist locally, try to get some information on the internet. Log on to the website for the Association of Pet Behaviour Counsellors (APBC) at www.apbc. co.uk. This is an international network of experienced and qualified pet behaviour counsellors, who, on referral from veterinary surgeons, treat behavioural problems in dogs. There is a list on the site showing UK clinics region by region. The APBC runs seminars and workshops on dog behaviour and training, and also sells books, videos and other products relating to the subject.

Hopefully, you will be able to find a behaviourist in your area who may be able to help you. It is unlikely that you will need this level of help with your German Shepherd Dog, but if you do have a serious behaviour problem, don't hesitate to get help. The earlier you get help, the more likely it is that the problem can be corrected.

SENIOR DOG TIP

Older Dogs and Problem Behaviours

Teaching a dog to stop doing something he's been doing for years is much, much harder than teaching him something new. With any behaviour, it is always easier to not let one get started than to try to change one that may have been going on for years. Depending on the problem, you may be able to replace the behaviour with another one. Every time your dog starts doing the unacceptable behaviour, distract him with something else he loves to do. That could be playing fetch or chewing on a treat-filled toy. If the behaviour is something serious like nipping, and has been growing worse, you may need a canine behaviourist.

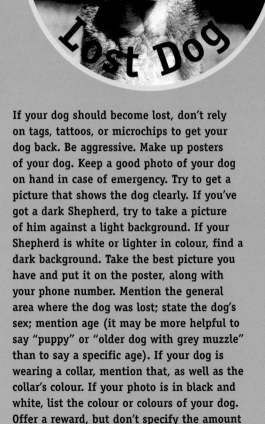

The Expert Knows
Lost Dog

If your dog should become lost, don't rely on tags, tattoos, or microchips to get your dog back. Be aggressive. Make up posters of your dog. Keep a good photo of your dog on hand in case of emergency. Try to get a picture that shows the dog clearly. If you've got a dark Shepherd, try to take a picture of him against a light background. If your Shepherd is white or lighter in colour, find a dark background. Take the best picture you have and put it on the poster, along with your phone number. Mention the general area where the dog was lost; state the dog's sex; mention age (it may be more helpful to say "puppy" or "older dog with grey muzzle" than to say a specific age). If your dog is wearing a collar, mention that, as well as the collar's colour. If your photo is in black and white, list the colour or colours of your dog. Offer a reward, but don't specify the amount on the poster.

Go door to door and ask your immediate neighbours to keep an eye out for your dog. Leave them a poster. Put posters on area bulletin boards, in veterinary surgeries, and at local stores. Recruit children. They'll probably cover more territory on foot than the adults in your neighbourhood, and they may be more apt to notice a dog. Don't encourage children to actually try to catch your dog. Ask them to come to you and lead you to the dog or to tell their parents and have them call you.

Call local police and dog wardens. There is also a chance your dog could have be hit by a car and taken to a vet. Keep calling. Check with your local rescue centre. Go in person and look at the dogs. Don't rely on phone calls and don't depend on having someone at a centre call you. Leave your name and phone number, of course, but also check in person. Notes can be lost, and centre personnel may change. They may have seen your dog and thought it was a mixed breed. Go to look at the dogs that have been picked up as strays. Go look at least every other day. Show the staff pictures of your dog.

If there's another rescue centre 20 or 30 miles away, visit it, too. German Shepherd Dogs can travel amazing distances. Also, if someone picked up your dog and dropped him off again, or lost him, he could end up farther away.

Run an ad in the lost and found column of your local newspaper. Ask your local radio stations to announce it. Many newspapers and radio stations are happy to run these kinds of public service announcements at no charge.

Chapter 8

Stepping Out

German Shepherd Dogs are so versatile, you can do just about any sport or activity with this breed. From showing to agility to obedience, there's nothing your GSD won't excel at, even if it's just having some fun in the backyard. And if you're going away on a well-deserved holiday, don't forget to take your best friend with you! Stepping out with your dog doesn't have to just mean for the day—a well-behaved GSD will make an excellent travelling companion.

Travelling With Your GSD

Holidays are more fun when everyone can go, but if you're travelling with your dog, you'll need to think ahead and do a little planning.

By Car

Make sure your dog enjoys travelling in a car. Take short, happy trips to get him used to car travel. Make sure the rides have good associations for the dog—don't let every trip end at the vet's.

Don't let your dog ride loose in the car. Just like human passengers, dogs need to be protected. And, in case of an accident, you don't want your dog escaping from the car and running loose on the motorway. Invest in a crate, or buy a harness that connects to a seat belt. If you choose the harness option, keep your dog in the back seat. Dogs, like small children, may be injured by front-seat air bags.

Think about the weather when you travel. Never leave your dog in a closed car. Even on a cool day, the temperature in a closed car can rise to killing temperatures. Dogs can die of heatstroke even if the car is parked in the shade (and remember, shade moves). A car parked in the shade may end up in direct sun in a couple of hours.

For his own safety, don't let your dog ride loose in the car.

Travelling With Children

Travelling with a child and a dog means more packing, but it may also mean fewer repetitions of "Are we there yet?" Give your child a job—he or she can check on the dog and make sure he's comfortable in his crate and has water. If your dog travels in a harness attached to the seat belt, your child can cuddle with the dog.

Depending on your child's age, he or she can also be responsible for walking the dog at service areas. Make sure your child is big enough and strong enough for this job. GSDs are strong dogs, and if he lunges after another dog or dashes after a squirrel, there could be an accident. It's another reason obedience lessons are a must for a GSD.

If your child is too small to walk the dog on his own, make a little loop on the lead at child height, or attach a smaller lead to the dog's collar, so your child can "walk" the dog with you.

Carry treats for both children and dog. If the treat is carrot sticks, they can share.

Remember, both dogs and children benefit from breaks. Plan to stop every two or three hours.

By Air

In the UK, it is relatively rare to take a pet dog on a plane, but with the PETS passport scheme, this option is becoming more popular.

Check with the airline for its rules and regulations regarding flying your dog. If you don't see your dog being put on the plane, have the counter agent call the ramp to make sure your dog is on board. At your destination, pick up your dog promptly.

Hotels and Motels

To find pet-friendly lodging, you can log on to www.petfriendly.co.uk for pet-friendly hotels in the UK or www.preferredplaces.co.uk, which lists holiday cottages where pets are welcome. For a website that gives details of pet-friendly hotels, cottages and camping, try www.dogsinvited.co.uk. Most hotel chains have websites so you can check various locations for their policies regarding pets. There are also guides for campgrounds that take pets. Rules will vary, and many times there is an extra fee for the dog.

Remember, not every hotel in a chain will have the same rules. Make sure you call first to see what the policies are in each case. Make your reservations ahead of time. Don't assume that you and your GSD will be welcome. Also, even if a hotel isn't listed as allowing pets, they may make an exception for an obedience-trained dog who will be in a crate, as long as they know ahead of time that you want to stay with them.

You don't have to leave your best friend behind—with a little planning your GSD can holiday with you.

What to Pack

Travelling with a dog is a lot like travelling with any member of the family. You'll need to pack your GSD a bag.

- Take along enough of your dog's food to last for the entire trip. Don't take a chance that you'll be able to buy your brand on the road. As happy as your dog will be to be with you on the trip, travel is still stressful, and a change of diet can lead to diarrhoea or vomiting.

- Carry water for your dog. If you'll just be on the road for a day or two, carry enough water from home for the entire trip. If the trip will be longer, top up the water jug with local water, gradually replacing the water from home.

- Don't forget dishes for that food and water.

- Carry plastic bags for clean up.

- Carry any medication your dog may be taking.

- Put together a doggy first aid kit. Include a blanket, disinfectant, and gauze pads. (See Chapter 5 for complete first aid information.)

- Think about where your dog will be sleeping. If you'll be in and out of motel rooms, consider buying a lightweight, folding travel crate to save you dragging a heavier crate in and out.

- Pack lots of extra towels. Towels work as bedding, and you'll need them for wiping off muddy paws and drying your dog if he's caught in the rain. Pack more towels than you think you'll need.

- Carry your dog's health records, and a contact number for your vet. If you are staying in one place, it may be worth finding out contact details for a local vet in case of an emergency.

- Take a toy or two and something for your dog to chew on. Just like people, dogs get bored. You might want to make a long line of clothesline with a clip on the end for your dog's collar so that you can throw a ball and he can get exercise chasing it without being loose.

- Make sure your dog is wearing identification tags. If you are going somewhere for a week or more, consider having a tag made with the local contact information on it. Or, put your mobile phone number on the tag.

- If you're staying in hotels, carry an extra sheet or two to spread on the beds. Vacuum cleaners will suck up the hair your dog leaves behind, but bedspreads are hard to wash and dog hairs tend to work their way into the weave. A sheet will protect the spread from both hair and muddy feet. If you're

only staying a night or two on your way to your destination and don't want to take up space with

SENIOR DOG TIP

Travelling With Older Dogs

Older dogs love to travel just as much as they did when they were younger, but remember that they'll need more frequent rest stops, and they won't be as agile as when they were more youthful.

Don't let an older dog bound from the car, but offer a bit of support in case their muscles have stiffened from the journey. An older dog is also more apt to suffer digestive upsets, so limit treats while travelling and make sure no new foods are introduced. If your older dog is on any medication, make sure you have enough to last the entire trip.

Your older dog won't have the stamina he had when he was younger. If your holidays have always included hiking, your dog may not be able to keep up. Take a short, easy walk with your dog, and then let him snooze away the day in your room while you tackle the mountain trails.

97

Stepping Out

extra sheets, ask housekeeping for sheets when you arrive. They'd rather wash the extra sheets than have to clean the bedspreads.

Sports and Other Activities

German Shepherd Dogs were bred to work and that, combined with their willingness to please, means you can do just about anything with your Shepherd. The more active your dog is, the better off he'll be physically and mentally; and the more you do with your dog, the closer the bond will be between the two of you. Choose an activity you'll enjoy, and your GSD will enjoy it, too!

Showing (Conformation)

If you bought your dog from the breeder, you were told that your dog was either "show quality" or "pet quality." Show quality means that your dog meets the standard for the breed; pet quality means there is some physical flaw that prevents you from showing him. Pet quality does not mean that your dog is any less healthy, but his bite may not be the required scissor bite, for instance.

If your dog is show quality, you can show him in conformation. Dogs at dog shows compete to win a much coveted Challenge Certificate. If a dog wins three Challenge Certificates under three different judges, he is made up into a champion and has the initials Ch. before his name.

Check with your training club, and see if they offer handling classes. This is the best way to learn what to do with your dog in the ring. To show your German Shepherd Dog in conformation, he will need to learn to stand quietly while the judge examines him. This examination includes teeth, so get your dog used to having his mouth opened. Your dog must also trot at your left side so that the judge can watch his movement to be sure he is sound and is moving as a German Shepherd Dog should.

Before you enter your first show, find a small exemption show. These shows are exempt from Kennel Club rules and will give you the chance to

If your dog is show quality, you can show him in conformation.

Your GSD can excel in events like herding(above) and agility (right).

Stepping Out

practice showing your GSD in a more informal environment. It's a good way to see how you and your dog will perform when in the ring with other dogs.

Performance Events

If conformation showing doesn't appeal to you, but you like the idea of competing with your Shepherd, consider one of the performance events. Performance events differ depending on where you live, but there are plenty to choose from. They include obedience, working trials, and agility.

- **Obedience**: There are several levels of obedience, starting at the basic pre-beginners level and working up to your dog becoming an Obedience Champion. Your dog is tested on heeling, sits, downs, stays, recalls, retrieving, and scentwork.

- **Rally**: This sport is not currently available in the UK, but it is a great introduction to obedience. In rally, you and your dog progress through from 10 to 20 stations. At each station is a card with instructions. For example, down, about turn, and stand for examination. Unlike obedience, in rally you can talk to your dog, and you can repeat an exercise without penalty.

- **Working Trials**: This is an event in which German Shepherd Dogs excel. It combines the elements of control, obedience, agility and nosework, and each level becomes increasingly more difficult. Obedience does not need to be as accurate as for Competitive Obedience, but it requires a high standard. Nosework includes following increasingly long and difficult tracks. Agility involves negotiating a scale and a long jump. The control elements involve manwork. The titles to aim for are Companion Dog, Utility Dog and Patrol Dog. For more information log on to www.workingtrials.co.uk.

- **Herding**: This sport is currently available only for German Shepherds in the United States. In herding, ducks, geese, sheep, goats, or cattle are used and the dog is judged on his ability to move the livestock through a course.

- **Agility**: Agility offers both fun and exercise. Courses and regulations vary, but generally, an agility course includes an A-frame, a teeter-totter, a dog walk, a tunnel, a closed tunnel, a pause table, and (depending on the level) weave poles. Dogs are timed, so the goal is to complete the course as quickly as possible with the fewest number of faults.

The regulations for all sports available in the UK are listed at www.the-kennel-club.org.uk. Find a class for obedience or a club that concentrates on agility to get your start.

Hiking

If competition doesn't appeal to you, there are still lots of ways to enjoy your GSD. If you enjoy hiking, your dog can learn to carry a backpack. Just remember to get your dog used to a backpack gradually and not to ask him to carry more than 20 percent of his weight, including the weight of the pack itself.

Wagon Pull

Your German Shepherd Dog can also be taught to pull a wagon. Just remember that with anything that requires pulling or carrying, start gradually, and don't add weight or ask your dog to pull until he is at least 18 months old. Have your vet check his hips and elbows to make sure he can participate in these activities without physical harm.

Search and Rescue

Search and Rescue is another area in which German Shepherd Dogs excel, but with Search and Rescue it's not a competition, and it's not for fun. It's a serious undertaking often with lives at stake. With their devotion to their owners, their willingness to work, and their keen noses, a Shepherd makes an excellent search and rescue dog.

In search and rescue, dogs are trained to follow scent working over a variety of terrains and in all weathers. Dogs are trained to find cadavers as well as victims still alive, and all of this requires regular training sessions.

Because of the amount of training involved, it's not generally something you can do on your own. Find a search and rescue group near you for training. The easiest way to do this is to log on to the website for the National Search and Rescue Dog Association at www.nsarda. org.uk. Dogs with a strong desire to play make good search and rescue dogs. They will work for the chance to play a game of fetch or for a treat.

Search and rescue teams are always on call, may have to travel many miles, and receive no pay, but the rewards of saving a life can make all the effort worthwhile.

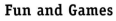

Fun and Games

For even more fun, play games with your dog. Put your dog on a sit-stay, or have another member of the family hold the dog. Run and hide, then call your dog, and let your dog find you.

Most German Shepherds love retrieving, so get a supply of tennis balls, and give your dog some exercise fetching the balls. You can use a flying disc, too, but remember that high leaps and twists can injure your dog, so keep the disc flying low.

Another fun game is to invert three plastic bowls and hide a treat under one of them. Tell your dog to find the treat. Or, hide a treat in another room and have your dog find it. Make it easy at first, placing the treat in the centre of the room, and then, gradually make the hiding place more difficult.

Invest in a book about how to teach your dog tricks. Your dog will enjoy learning, and you'll have fun, too. My father taught his dog to "play dead" and then to leap up barking at the mention of the dogcatcher.

You can always have a great time right in your own backyard with your GSD.

Dogs, just like human athletes, need to be in top condition, and they need to take precautions against injury. That's one of the reasons that dogs may not compete in agility until they are 18 months old. It's to make sure that they are fully developed. Many owners of larger dogs like the GSD wait until the dog is 18 months to two years old before competing. Training can begin before then, of course, but training is less stressful than competition.

Don't expect your dog to be an outstanding athlete on the weekend if he never gets any exercise during the week. Condition your dog by jogging or with practice sessions.

Before any performance event, stretch your dog and get him warmed up. Asking your dog to put his paws on your shoulders will give him a good stretch. Walk your dog around to help loosen his muscles, especially if he's been travelling in his crate for an hour or more. Trot your dog to continue warming him up.

After a competition, make sure there's plenty of water for your dog. It's easy for a dog to overheat so get him into the shade, and offer water after that agility run. At many performance events, the sponsors will supply wading pools full of water for cooling down the contestants. Most dogs enjoy the water and will lie down in it on their own.

Resources

Associations and Organisations

Breed and Kennel Clubs

American Kennel Club (AKC)
5580 Centerview Drive
Raleigh, NC 27606
Telephone: (919) 233-9767
Fax: (919) 233-3627
E-mail: info@akc.org
www.akc.org

British Association of German Shepherd Dogs
E-mail: bagsd@freeuk.com
http://www.bagsd.net/index.htm

British GSD Training Club
18 Appledore Grove,
Sutton Leach, St. Helen's,
Merseyside WA9 4NG
Telephone: 01744 810100

Canadian Kennel Club (CKC)
89 Skyway Avenue, Suite 100
Etobicoke, Ontario M9W 6R4
Telephone: 416 675 5511
Fax: 416 675 6506
E-mail: information@ckc.ca
www.ckc.ca

Federation Cynologique Internationale (FCI)
Secretariat General de la FCI
Place Albert 1er,
13B – 6530 Thuin
Belqique
www.fci.be

German Shepherd Dog League of Great Britain (GSDL)
Warrant Wood Farmhouse
Ternhill, Market Drayton,
Shropshire TF9 2JA
Telephone: 01630 638540
E-mail: enquiries@gsdleague.co.uk
www.gsdleague.co.uk

GSD Club of the United Kingdom
Telephone: 01302 751743

The Kennel Club
1 Clarges Street
London W1J 8AB
Telephone: 0870 606 6750
Fax: 0207 518 1058
www.the-kennel-club.org.uk

United Kennel Club (UKC)
100 E. Kilgore Road
Kalamazoo, MI 49002-5584
Telephone: 269 343 9020
Fax: 269 343 7037
E-mail: pbickell@ukcdogs.com
www.ukcdogs.com

Verein Für Deutsche Schåferhunder (SV)
Håuptgeschaftsstelle
Steinerne Furt 71
86167 Ausburg, Germany
Telephone: 0821 740020
Fax: 0821 74002 903
E-mail: info@schaeferhunde.de
www.schaeferhunde.de/sv_start_english.htm

German Shepherd Dog

White and Long Coat Shepherd Society (WLCSS)
Telephone: 01525 718300
E-mail: petkargsd@yahoo.co.uk
http://www.walcss.50megs.com

Pet Sitters
National Association of Registered Petsitters
www.dogsit.com

UK Petsitters
Telephone: 01902 41789
www.ukpetsitter.com

Dog Services UK
www.dogservices.co.uk

Rescue Organisations and Animal Welfare Groups
British Veterinary AssociationAnimal Welfare Foundation (BVA AWF)
7 Mansfield Street
London W1G 9NQ
Telephone: 0207 636 6541
Fax: 0207 436 2970
Email: bva-awf@bva.co.uk
www.bva-awf.org.uk/about

Royal Society for the Prevention of Cruelty to Animals (RSPCA)
Telephone: 0870 3335 999
Fax: 0870 7530 284
www.rspca.org.uk

Scottish Society for the Prevention of Cruelty to Animals (SSPCA)
Braehead Mains, 603 Queensferry Road

Edinburgh EH4 6EA
Telephone: 0131 339 0222
Fax: 0131 339 4777
Email: enquiries@scottishspca.org
www.scottishspca.org/about

Sports
Agility Club UK
www.agilityclub.co.uk

British Flyball Association
PO Box 109
Petersfield GU32 1XZ
Telephone: 01753 620110
Fax: 01726 861079
Email: bfa@flyball.org.uk
www.flyball.org.uk

British Schutzhund Association
15 Measham Road
Donisthorpe Swadlincote
Derbyshire DE12 7QQ
E-mail: nexcess@schutzhund.fsnet.co.uk
http://www.schutzhund.fsnet.co.uk/.

Canine Freestyle Federation, Inc.
Secretary: Brandy ClymireE-Mail:
secretary@canine-freestyle.org
www.canine-freestyle.org

International Agility Link (IAL)
Global Administrator: Steve
DrinkwaterE-mail: yunde@powerup.
auwww.agilityclick.com/~ial

World Canine Freestyle Organisation
P.O. Box 350122Brooklyn, NY 11235-
2525Telephone: (718) 332-8336www.
worldcannefreestyle.org

Therapy

Pets As Therapy
3 Grange Farm Cottages
Wycombe Road, Saunderton
Princes Risborough
Bucks HP27 9NS
Telephone: 0870 977 0003
Fax: 0870 706 2562
www.petsastherapy.org

Therapy Dogs International (TDI)
88 Bartley Road
Flanders, NJ 07836
Telephone: (973) 252-9800
Fax: (973) 252-7171
E-mail: tdi@gti.net
www.tdi-dog.org

Training and Behaviour

Association of Pet Dog Trainers (APDT)
PO Box 17
Kempsford GL7 4W7
Telephone: 01285 810811

Association of Pet Behaviour Counsellors
PO Box 46
Worcester WR8 9YS
Telephone: 01386 751151
Fax: 01386 750743
Email: info@apbc.org.uk
www.apbc.org.uk

Association of British Veterinary Acupuncturists (ABVA)
66A Easthorpe, Southwell
Nottinghamshire NG25 0HZ
Email: jonnyboyvet@hotmail.com
www.abva.co.uk

Association of Chartered Physiotherapists Specialising in Animal Therapy (ACPAT)
52 Littleham Road
Exmoouth, Devon EX8 2QJ
Telephone/Fax: 01395 270648
Email: bexsharples@hotmail.com
www.acpat.org.uk

British Association of Homoeopathic Veterinary Surgeons
Alternative Veterinary
Medicine Centre
Chinham House
Stanford in the Vale
Oxfordshire SN7 8NQ
Email: enquiries@bahvs.com
www.bahvs.com

British Association of Veterinary Opthalmologists (BAVO)
Email: hjf@vetspecialists.co.uk
Email: secretary@bravo.org.uk
www.bravo.oprg.uk

British Small Animal Veterinary Association (BSAVA)
Woodrow House, 1 Telford Way
Waterwells Business Park
Quedgley, Gloucester GL2 2AB
Telephone: 01452 726700
Fax: 01452 726701
Email: customerservices@bsava.com
www.bsava.com

British Veterinary Association (BVA)
7 Mansfield Street
LondonW1G 9NQ
Telephone: 020 7636 6541

Fax: 020 7436 2970
E-mail: bvahq@bva.co.uk
www.bva.co.uk

British Veterinary Hospitals Association (BHVA)
Station Bungalow
Main Road, Stockfield
Northumberland NE43 7HJ
Telephone: 07966 901619
Fax: 07813 915954
Email: office@bvha.org.uk
www.BVHA.org.uk

Royal College of Veterinary Surgeons (RCVS)
Belgravia House, 62-64 Horseferry Road
London SW1P 2AF
Telephone: 0207 222 2001
Fax: 0207 222 2004
Email: admin@rcvs.org.uk
www.rcvs.org.uk

Publications

Newspapers and Magazines

Dog World Ltd
Somerfield House
Wotton Road, Ashford
Kent TN23 6LW
Telephone: 01233 621877
Fax: 01233 645669

Dogs Monthly
Ascot House, High Street,
Ascot, Berkshire SL5 7JG
Telephone: 0870 730 8433
Fax: 0870 730 8431
Email: admin@rtc-associates.freeserve.co.uk
www.corsini.co.uk/dogsmonthly

Dogs Today
Town Mill, Bagshot Road
Chobham, Surrey GU24 8BZ
Telephone: 01276 858880
Fax: 01276 858860
Email: enquiries@dogstodaymagazine.co.uk
www.dogstodaymagazine.co.uk

Kennel Gazette
Kennel Club
1 Clarges Street
London W1J 8AB
Telephone: 0870 606 6750
Fax: 0207 518 1058
www.the-kennel-club.co.uk

K9 Magazine
21 High Street
Warsop
Nottinghamshire NG20 0AA
Telephone: 0870 011 4114
Fax: 0870 706 4564
Email: mail@k9magazine.com
www.k9magazine.com

League Review
German Shepherd Dog League of Great Britain (GSDL)
Warrant Wood Farmhouse
Ternhill, Market Drayton
Shropshire TF9 2JA
Telephone: 01630 638540
E-mail: enquiries@gsdleague.co.uk
www.gsdleague.co.uk

Our Dogs
Our Dogs Publishing
5 Oxford Road
Station Approach
Manchester M60 1SX
www.ourdogs.co.uk

107

Resources

Your Dog
Roebuck House
33 Broad Street
Stamford
Lincolnshire PE9 1RB
Telephone: 01780 766199
Fax: 01780 766416

Books
The Super Simple Guide to Housetraining
Anderson, Teoti.
Neptune, NJ: TFH Publications, 2004.

Good Dogkeeping
Morgan, Diane.
Neptune, NJ: TFH Publications, 2005.

How to Behave So Your Dog Behaves
Yin, Sophia, DVM
Neptune, NJ: TFH Publications, 2004.

Mini Encyclopedia of Dog Training &
Behaviour
Tennant, Colin
Dorking, Surrey: Interpet Publishing,
2005

What If My Dog...?
Evans, Jim
Dorking, Surrey: Interpet Publishing,
2006

Websites
Herding on the Web
www.herdingontheweb.com)
This site covers every topic related to
training a dog to herd. The extensive list
of media resources, international clubs,
and herding techniques will help GSD
owners learn to teach their companion
this skill.

German Shepherd World
www.gsdworld.net)
This site is an international forum that
allows GSD owners from every part
of the globe to connect and to discuss
every topic relating to their beloved
GSDs, including diet, nutrition, training,
health issues, showing, and more...

German Shepherd Dog

Index

A

accessories and clothing, 47-48, 48!
acupuncture, 65-66
adopting the older dog, 19
adult dogs, feeding of, 33t
age-appropriate feeding, chart, 33t
aggression, 85, 89
agility competition, 99!, 100
air travel, 95
allergies, vaccinations and, 57
alternative medical therapies, 65-67
American Kennel Club (AKC), 7
animal behaviourists, 89-90
annual medical exams, 53
apartment living and the German Shepherd Dog, 11
associations and organisations, 104-105

B

baby gates, 19
BARF diets, 29-30
barking, 84-85
bathing, 41-43, 42!
beds and bedding, 17-18
begging, 27
bloat, 57-58
Blount, Wendy, 32
body language and communication, 75
body, 8-9
bones and joints
  degenerative myelopathy and, 58
  hip dysplasia in, 58-59
bones in diet, 29-30
Bordetella, 54
bowls for food and water, 18-19, 19!
Braustein, Shirlee, 12
breed clubs, 104
brushes and brushing, 40-41, 40!

C

cancer, 61
canned dog food, 26-27
car travel, 94
champion German Shepherd Dogs, 12
chewing, 85-87
children and the German Shepherd Dog, 10!, 11, 21, 29, 46, 53, 70, 70!, 71, 87, 95
chiropractic, 66
choking, 62-63
clicker training, 81
coat and skin, 7-8. *See also* grooming
  shedding and, 40, 49
collars, 21-22, 43-44
colour, 8
Come command, 76, 76!
commercial dog food, 26-29
communicating with your German Shepherd Dog, 75
conformation showing, 98-99, 98!
coronavirus, 54-55
crates, 16-17, 16!
Crotius, Kendall, 49

D

day care for dogs, 22
degenerative myelopathy, 58
dental care, 46-47, 47!
diarrhoea, 62
digging, 87
distemper, 54, 55
dog food, 26-29
Down command, 78-79
dry food 27
drying your wet German Shepherd Dog, 43
Duncan, Lee, 12
dysplasia, hip, 58-59

E

ear care, 44
emergency medical treatment, 61-62
Eustis, Dorothy Harris, 7

exercise pens, 18
exercise requirements, 10, 23
eye care, 44

F

feeding, 25-37
  adult dogs, 33t
  age-appropriate, 33t
  bloat and, 57-58
  bones in, 29-30
  bowls for, 18-19, 19!
  canned foods in, 26-27
  choosing the right food for, 28-29
  commercial dog food in, 26-29
  dry food in, 27
  home-cooked meals in, 30-32
  inflammatory bowel disease (IBD) and, 59
  label contents of dog foods in, 27-28
  obesity and, 34-36
  puppies, 33t
  raw or BARF diets in, 29-30
  scheduled vs. free-feeding in, 34
  semi-moist foods in, 27
  table manners and, 27
  toxic or poisons foods/materials in, 37
  treats and, 36
  variety of foods in, 32, 34
  veteran dogs and, 30, 33t
  vitamin and mineral supplements in, 32
Firestone, Jane A., 12
first-aid for your German Shepherd Dog, 61-62
flea control, 60
flower essence therapy, 67
Frank, Morris, 7
free-feeding vs. scheduled meals, 34

G

games to play with your German Shepherd Dog, 102

gates, 19
Germany and the German Shepherd Dog, 6-7
grooming, 39-49
  accessories and clothing in, 47-48, 48!
  bathing in, 41-43, 42!
  brushes and brushing in, 40-41, 40!
  dental care and, 46-47, 47!
  drying in, 43
  ear care and, 44
  eye care and, 44
  health check during, 44
  nail care and, 44-46, 45!
  professional groomers for, 47
  shedding and, 40, 49
  tables for, 43
  tools and supplies for, 19-20, 41
  veteran dogs and, 48
grooming tables, 43
guarding instinct, 6-7. *See also* Schutzhund trials
guide dogs, 7

H
harnesses, 21
head, 8
health issues, 51-67
  acupuncture in, 65-66
  allergic reactions to vaccines and, 57
  annual check-ups, 53
  bloat in, 57-58
  Bordetella in, 54
  cancer in, 61
  chiropractic in, 66
  choking in, 62-63
  coronavirus in, 54-55
  degenerative myelopathy in, 58
  dental care and, 46-47, 47!
  diarrhoea in, 62
  distemper in, 54, 55
  ear care and, 44
  emergency medical treatment and, 61-62
  eye care and, 44
  first-aid in, 61-62
  flea control in, 60
  flower essence therapy in, 67

grooming and, as health check, 44
hepatitis in, 54, 55
herbal medicine in, 67
hip dysplasia in, 58-59
holistic/alternative medical therapies in, 65-67
home boarding, 22
homeopathy in, 67
housesoiling as, 87-88
inflammatory bowel disease (IBD) in, 59
insurance for, 59
leptospirosis in, 54, 55
Lyme disease in, 55
muzzling your dog in, 64-65
neutering and spaying in, 56
obesity and, 34-36
parainfluenza in, 54
parvovirus in, 54, 55, 57
poisoning in, 62
puppies and, first vet visits for, 52-53
rabies in, 54, 57
sports safety and, 103
temperature in, 62
tick control and removal in, 60
transporting injured animals in, 65
vaccinations and, 53-57
vet selection in, 52
veteran dogs and, 62, 67
vitamin and mineral supplements in, 32
vomiting in, 62
health/medical insurance for pets, 59
hepatitis, 54, 55
herbal medicine, 67
herding competition, 99!, 100
herding instinct, 6-7
hiking with your German Shepherd Dog, 100
hip dysplasia, 58-59
history of the German Shepherd Dog, 6-7
holistic therapies, 65-67
Hollywood and the German Shepherd Dog, 7, 12

home-cooked meals, 30-32
homeopathy, 67
hotel and motel accommodations, 95
housetraining accidents, 87-88
housetraining, 71-74
  housetraining accidents and, 87-88
  paper training and, 74

I
identification tags, 20
inflammatory bowel disease (IBD), 59
insurance, medical, 59
Internet resources, 108

J
jumping up, 88

K
Knitting with Dog Hair, 49

L
label contents of dog foods, 27-28
leads, 21-22
leptospirosis, 54, 55
living with a German Shepherd Dog, 10
lost dogs, 91
Lyme disease, 55

M
microchipping, 20
Montgomery, Anne, 49
Moses, James, 12
movement and gait, 9
muzzling your dog, 64-65
myelopathy, degenerative, 58

N
nail care, 44-46, 45!
neutering, 56
New Choices in Natural Healing for Dogs and Cats, 67
nipping, 89

German Shepherd Dog

O

obedience competition, 100
obesity, 34–36
other pets and the German Shepherd Dog, 11-12, 70!

P

paper training, 74
parainfluenza, 54
parvovirus, 54, 55, 57
pet sitters, 104
poisoning, 37, 62
police dogs, 20!
Pottle, Cappy, 12
problem behaviours, 83–91
    aggression as, 85, 89
    animal behaviourists for, 89–90
    barking as, 84–85
    chewing as, 85–87
    digging as, 87
    housetraining accidents as, 87–88
    jumping up as, 88
    nipping as, 89
    separation anxiety as, 85
    table manners and begging as, 27
    veteran dogs and, 90
professional groomers, 47
Propps, Jannettia Brodsgaard, 12
publications, 107–108
pulling competition, 100, 102
puppies
    chewing and, 85–87
    feeding of, 33*t*
    housetraining and, 71-74
    neutering, 56
    paper training and, 74
    socialisation of, 70–71
    vaccinations and, 53–57
    vet visits for, 52–53

R

rabies, 54, 57
rally obedience, 100
raw or BARF diets, 29–30
rescue organisations and animal welfare, 104–105
resources, 104–107
Rin Tin Tin, 7, 12

Rinty for Kids Foundation, A (ARFkids), 12

S

scheduled vs. free-feeding, 34
schedules for your German Shepherd Dog, 17
Schutzhund trials, 6–7. *See also* guarding instinct
search-and-rescue dogs, 10
semi-moist foods, 27
separation anxiety, 85
service dogs, 12, 101
shedding, 40, 49
showing (conformation), 98–99, 98!
Sit command, 76–77, 77!
size and weight, 7
socialisation, 10, 70–71
spinning dog fur into yarn, 49
sports associations, 105
sports safety, 103
Stay command, 77–78, 78!

T

tattoos for ID, 20–21
temperament and personality, 9–10
temperature, normal, 62
therapy dogs, 105
tick control and removal, 60
today's German Shepherd Dog, 7
toxic or poisons foods/materials, 37
toys, 22–23
tracking competition, 100
training, 10, 69–83, 105–106
    body language and communication in, 75
    clicker training in, 81
    Come command in, 76, 76!
    Down command and, 78–79
    housetraining in, 71–74
    paper training and, 74
    problem behaviours and. *See* problem behaviours
    Sit command in, 76-77, 77!
    socialisation in, 70–71
    Stay command in, 77–78, 78!

table manners and, 27
treats and, 74
tricks to teach your German Shepherd Dog and, 80–81, 80!
veteran dogs and, 78
walking with your German Shepherd Dog and, 79–80, 79!
transporting injured animals, 65
travelling with your German Shepherd Dog, 94–98
Travelling with Your Pet, 95
treats, 36, 74
tricks to teach your German Shepherd Dog, 80–81, 80!

U

United States and the German Shepherd Dog, 7

V

vaccinations, 53–57
vet selection, 52, 106
veteran dogs, 9
    adoption of, adapting to a new home and, 19
    feeding, 30, 33*t*
    grooming of, 48
    health issues and health care for, 62, 67
    problem behaviours in, 90
    training of, 78
    travelling with, 97
vitamin and mineral supplements, 32
vomiting, 62
von Stephanitz, Max, 6

W

wagon pull competition, 100
walking with your German Shepherd Dog, 79–80, 79!
websites of interest, 108
white German Shepherd Dog, 8

Dedication

For the Smith Family: Dick, Shirley, and Dale

About the Author

Susan Ewing has been "in dogs" since 1977 and has had Pembroke Welsh Corgis since 1983. She owned and operated a boarding kennel for four years and enjoys showing and participating in various performance events. She is affiliated with the Dog Writers Association of America and the Cat Writers' Association, of which she is treasurer. Susan has been writing professionally since 1964 for newspapers, magazines, and radio. She is the author of *The Pembroke Welsh Corgi: Family Friend and Farmhand* and *A New Owner's Guide to Pembroke Welsh Corgis.* Her column, "The Pet Pen," is in *The Post-Journal* (Jamestown, NY) every Saturday. She currently lives in Mesa, Arizona, with her husband, Jim, and two Corgis, Griffin and Rhiannon.

Photo Credits

American Dog Rescue Association: 101
Chris Anderson (Shutterstock): 82
Chris Bence (Shutterstock): 36 (bowl)
Andraz Cerar (Shutterstock): 92
Tara Darling: 99 (top)
Sasha Davas (Shutterstock): 13 (bottom)
Felix Fernandez Gonzalez (Shutterstock): 96
Naomi Hasegawa (Shutterstock): 38
Nicole Hrustyk (Shutterstock): 88
David Huntely (Shutterstock): 19
Cindy Jenkins (Shutterstock): 20
Emily Jindra (Shutterstock): 4
Peter Larsson (Shutterstock): 63
Malle (Shutterstock): 48
Mary Anne Miller: 12
Maxim (Shutterstock): 13

Humberto Ortega (Shutterstock): 23
Jason X Pacheco (Shutterstock): 80
Stephanie Schoenbein (Shutterstock): 50
Dimitri Sherman (Shutterstock): 18
Author photo courtesy of Ed Tomassini
Claudia Steiniger (Shutterstock): 42
Michaela Steininger (Shutterstock): 84
Vendla Stockdale (Shutterstock): 31
Judith Strom: 70
April Turner (Shutterstock): 33
Tonis Valing (Shutterstock): 14, 68
Alan Wesley (Shutterstock): 49, 58

All other photos courtesy of Isabelle Francais
Cover photo: Roger Roman (Shutterstock)